THE SOFT ATLAS
OF AMSTERDAM

JAN ROTHUIZEN

THE SOFT ATLAS OF AMSTERDAM

For those moments where you miss Amsterdam! Just come back soon!! With love, Don & Tes.

Nieuw Amsterdam *Uitgevers*

The original Dutch edition – *De zachte Atlas van Amsterdam* – first appeared in 2009 and is now in its 7th edition. This *Soft Atlas of Amsterdam* is not a translation of the Dutch edition, despite the title and even though some of the drawings are the same.

© JAN ROTHUIZEN 2014
ALL RIGHTS RESERVED
DESIGN: SOERAYA SIEMONS
TRANSLATIONS: SAM HERMAN
EDITING: ESTHER OTTENS & WYBRAND SCHEFFER
NUR 400/640
ISBN 978 90 468 1639 4
WWW.JANROTHUIZEN.NL
WWW.NIEUWAMSTERDAM.NL

CONTENTS

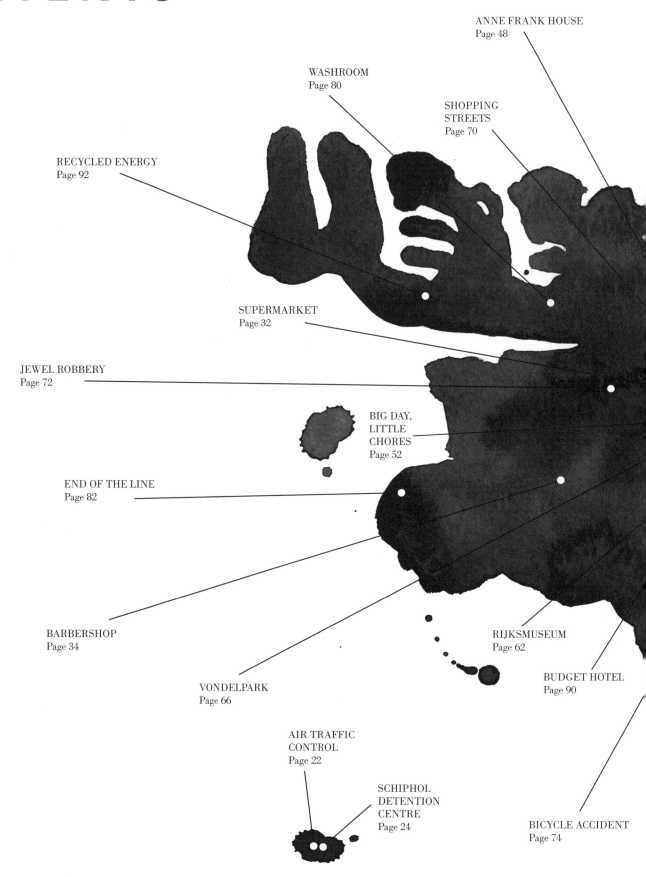

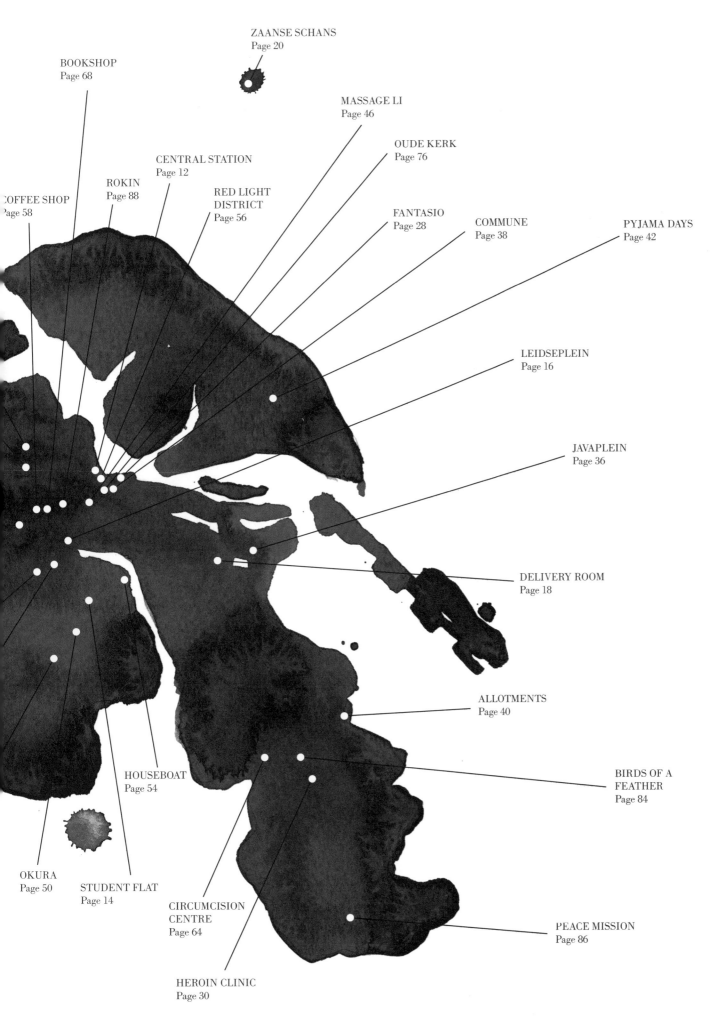

INTRODUCTION

A curious effect of habit is to make the familiar seem invisible. So some people take holidays. They travel not just to get away; they travel to be able to see the place they live in from a different angle when they get back. Another way to get a new perspective is to chart what you see and know. Close your eyes and imagine walking on one of your regular routes. The amount of information you have stored in your brain will come as a surprise.

The drawings in this volume are perhaps best described as written maps or graphic reportages. That is my best description yet. When I became an artist I knew that the confined space of a studio was not for me. I gradually found that my best way of being an artist consisted of walking around the city streets and meeting people. I wandered around cities like Cairo, New York, Guangzhou and Beirut. Strangely, my work didn't treat the city I was born and raised in. I decided it was time to make a book about Amsterdam. It was difficult at first: the city is such an integral part of me that I found it hard to see what I was looking at. I realised that my Amsterdam was just a small part of the city; my routes tended to be the same, and so were the people and places. It struck me that I had actually been to Manhattan more often than to Southeast Amsterdam.

The title of this atlas refers to *Soft City*, a book written in 1974 by British author *Jonathan Raban*. His idea is that the city is where the solid concrete reality of buildings and asphalt meets the malleable, subjective experience and expectation of the people who live and work there. When I chose the title for my book I had no idea how appropriate the word soft was for the Amsterdam that I have come to know in the last years.

Jan Rothuizen
march 2014

CIT
GAT

INBOUND

CITY GATES

In the 17th century, Amsterdam was surrounded by a wall with gates. Today's Amsterdam no longer starts where the houses end. A city gate can be in the middle of a street and a building. Anywhere where people can enter and leave the city.

The area around Central Station, the behaviour of taxi drivers, the atmosphere in the streets and the bars: it sets the scene for the city. That's why Amsterdam's city council wants to cut prostitution in the red light district, and to replace souvenir shops, fast-food outlets and coffee shops with chic design and fashion shops and restaurants.

ON A SATURDAY

STATION

BACK

16:20 IN A GOOD MOOD.

MEN WITH BENIGN SMILES: BELIEVERS (DOUBTLESS)

PEEEEEP! PEEEEEP (BRAKES)

BUILD ING SITE

ENGLISH - SPEAKING MEN WITH BANNER: WHERE WILL YOU SPEND ETERNITY! WITH GOD OR SATAN?

COFFEE-HOUSE

TOURIST INFO

TERRACE

OLD WOODEN HOUSE (NOSTALGIC) PAINTED WHITE, HYPER MODERN INSIDE

PEDESTRIAN BRIDGE

* FRIEND CALLS TO ASK IF I CAN MAKE IT TO A GALLERY OPENING. ITS THE START OF THE SEASON.

HER NAME IS JETSKE

A DISTANT MEMORY COMING OUT OF THE STATION WITH MY MOTHER THERE'S A MASSIVE FIRE BEHIND OR BESIDE THE CHURCH THIS RED NEON CROSS STANDS OUT AGAINST THE FLAMES AND SMOKE. EVER SINCE I'VE AVOIDED RELIGION.

HOTEL WHERE (DRUGGED) TRUMPET LEGEND CHET BAKER FELL FROM WINDOW (DEAD)

nh HOTEL (NEW AND UGLY)

OLDEST WOODEN HOUSE IN THE CITY

STATUE OF

ST OLOFS CHAPEL WAS FOR NORWEGIAN SAILORS

ST NICOLAS'S CHURCH OFFICIAL NAME: ST NICOLAS IN THE RAMPART

STEP GABLE

ONE

ST.

OUDE ZIJDS CANAL

MORITO - YA JAPANESE RESTAURANT (NICE ATMOSPHERE)

FORMER BROTHEL NOW AN AMSTERDAM FASHION EXHIBITION)

TWO THIRTY- SOMETHINGS IN COLOURFUL RAINCOATS WITH A BRIEFCASE SPORTING A BAANTJER TV DETECTIVE LOGO

"DISCOVER THE RED LIGHT DISTRICT AND FOLLOW THE (DETECTIVE) CLUES" (I FOUND ON INTERNET LATER) THE TOUR TAKES 5 HOURS € 32.50 OPTIONAL EXTRA 3 COURSE MEAL FOR € 19.50 EXTRA!

ZEEDIJK WAS ONCE A NO-GO AREA NOW MOTHERS AND DAUGHTERS FROM THE PROVINCE WALK HERE... AND OFFICE PARTIES LOTS OF ASIAN FOOD

I'M EATING A ROLL WITH A (MYSTERY MEAT) CROQUET. MMM DELICIOUS

FEBO (FERDINAND BOL) IS A STREET NAMED AFTER A GOLDEN AGE PAINTER

THEY'RE ALL WEARING TO A (RED) ROSE PINNED TO THEIR COAT. (IT'S A GIRLS DAY OUT TOUR. "PEEKING AT THE WHORES" (€ 13.50 EACH)

A WOMAN (CHUBBY) IS STANDING HERE SURROUNDED BY TEN BRIGHT YOUNG WOMEN SHE TELLS THEM THAT WOMEN ENJOY SEX TOO "WELL LETS BE HONEST" I SUSPECT SHE WAS ONCE A PROSTITUTE HERSELF AND NOW LEADS A TOUR OF THE RED LIGHT DISTRICT. I HEAR THE NUMBER 33 MENTIONED - SHE MEANS 33 CUSTOMERS A DAY! THE WOMEN GIGGLE AT THE IDEA. THE FORMER HOOKER KEEPS A STRAIGHT FACE AND OFFERS A COMPARISON THAT MAKES THE NUMBER SEEM MORE MUNDANE SOMETHING LIKE A BAKER SELLS LOTS OF BREAD TOO.

13

DOESN'T HE?

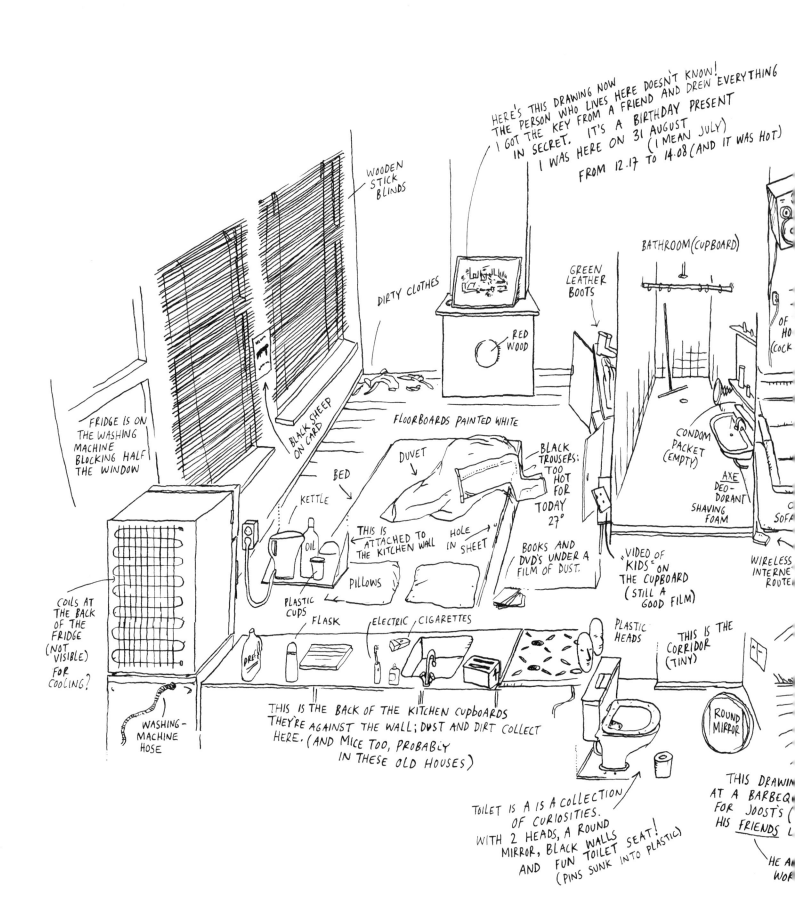

HERE'S THIS DRAWING NOW
THE PERSON WHO LIVES HERE DOESN'T KNOW!
I GOT THE KEY FROM A FRIEND AND DREW EVERYTHING
IN SECRET. IT'S A BIRTHDAY PRESENT
I WAS HERE ON 31 AUGUST
(I MEAN JULY)
FROM 12.17 TO 14.08 (AND IT WAS HOT)

WOODEN
STICK
BLINDS

DIRTY CLOTHES

RED
WOOD

GREEN
LEATHER
BOOTS

BATHROOM (CUPBOARD)

OF
HO
(COCK

FRIDGE IS ON
THE WASHING
MACHINE
BLOCKING HALF
THE WINDOW

BLACK SHEEP
ON CARD

FLOORBOARDS PAINTED WHITE

DUVET

BED

KETTLE

THIS IS
ATTACHED TO
THE KITCHEN WALL

HOLE
IN SHEET

BLACK
TROUSERS;
TOO
HOT
FOR
TODAY
27°

CONDOM
PACKET
(EMPTY)

AXE
DEO-
DORANT
SHAVING
FOAM

SOFA

WIRELESS
INTERNE
ROUTE

OIL

PILLOWS

BOOKS AND
DVD'S UNDER A
FILM OF DUST.

"VIDEO OF
KIDS" ON
THE CUPBOARD
(STILL A
GOOD FILM)

COILS AT
THE BACK
OF THE
FRIDGE
(NOT
VISIBLE)
FOR
COOLING?

PLASTIC
CUPS

FLASK

ELECTRIC CIGARETTES

PLASTIC
HEADS

THIS IS THE
CORRIDOR
(TINY)

WASHING-
MACHINE
HOSE

THIS IS THE BACK OF THE KITCHEN CUPBOARDS
THEY'RE AGAINST THE WALL; DUST AND DIRT COLLECT
HERE. (AND MICE TOO, PROBABLY
IN THESE OLD HOUSES)

ROUND
MIRROR

TOILET IS A IS A COLLECTION
OF CURIOSITIES.
WITH 2 HEADS, A ROUND
MIRROR, BLACK WALLS
AND FUN TOILET SEAT!
(PINS SUNK INTO PLASTIC)

THIS DRAWIN
AT A BARBEQ
FOR JOOST'S (
HIS FRIENDS L

HE A
WO

While half the tenants in Amsterdam rent
subsidised housing, on average people
wait eight or ten years before being allo-
cated. The housing market is gridlocked,
since people stay put once they get a
house, instead of moving on when they
start to earn more: it's cheaper to rent.

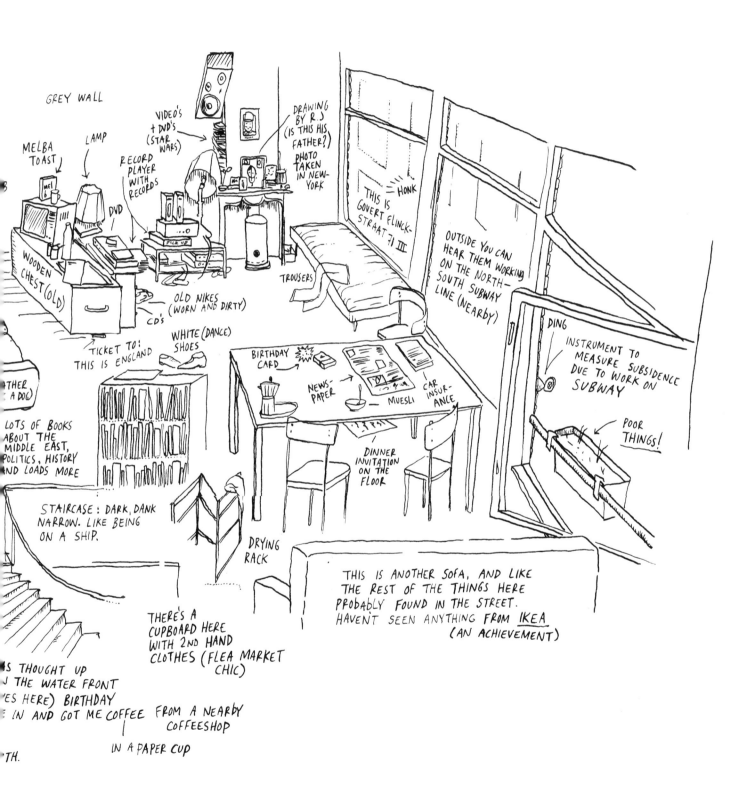

GREY WALL

MELBA TOAST

LAMP

VIDEO'S + DVD'S (STAR WARS)

RECORD PLAYER WITH RECORDS

DVD

DRAWING BY R.J. (IS THIS HIS FATHER?)

PHOTO TAKEN IN NEW YORK

PICK UP

WOODEN CHEST (OLD)

OLD NIKES (WORN AND DIRTY)

CD'S

TROUSERS

THIS IS GOVERT FLINCK-STRAAT 71 III

HONK

OUTSIDE YOU CAN HEAR THEM WORKING ON THE NORTH-SOUTH SUBWAY LINE (NEARBY)

DING

INSTRUMENT TO MEASURE SUBSIDENCE DUE TO WORK ON SUBWAY

POOR THINGS!

TICKET TO: THIS IS ENGLAND

WHITE (DANCE) SHOES

BIRTHDAY CARD

NEWS-PAPER

MUESLI

CAR INSUR-ANCE

...THER ...A DOG)

LOTS OF BOOKS ABOUT THE MIDDLE EAST, POLITICS, HISTORY AND LOADS MORE

DINNER INVITATION ON THE FLOOR

STAIRCASE: DARK, DANK NARROW. LIKE BEING ON A SHIP.

DRYING RACK

THERE'S A CUPBOARD HERE WITH 2ND HAND CLOTHES (FLEA MARKET CHIC)

THIS IS ANOTHER SOFA, AND LIKE THE REST OF THE THINGS HERE PROBABLY FOUND IN THE STREET. HAVEN'T SEEN ANYTHING FROM IKEA (AN ACHIEVEMENT)

...S THOUGHT UP
...J THE WATER FRONT
...ES HERE) BIRTHDAY
... IN AND GOT ME COFFEE FROM A NEARBY COFFEESHOP

IN A PAPER CUP

...TH.

21:08
KIDS STARTING THE
NIGHT WITH A PLASTIC
COKE BOTTLE, WITH
WHISKEY

NICE AND
CHEAP

PISSING
AGAINST
THE
RAAMGRACHT
POLICE
STATION
WALL

TRANSPORTER
POLICE VAN TO DRIVE
SUSPECTS AWAY QUICKLY
BEFORE THE PUBLIC START
TO GET INVOLVED, ESPECIALLY
STREET LAWYERS

CAFÉ MOKUM
SHOWS LIVE
SOCCER FOR FANS
BANNED FROM THE
STADIUM

CAFÉ
MOKUM

TONIGHT,
AMSTERDAM
DANCE
EVENT
(BOOM
BOOM)

BOOM
CHIGACO

(CLASSIC)
OYSTER
BAR

TRADITIONAL
DUTCH BARS
DISGUISED AS AN
IRISH PUB   WHY?

THREE
SISTERS

IRISH PUB

CINE
CENTER
CINEMA

SPASH
SUGAR
FACTORY
DANCE
CLUB

LIJNBAANS
GRACHT

MELK-
WEG

TONIGHT AN AFRICAN BAND,
(ALL MEN)
LADYSMITHBLACKMAMBAZO

FROM
PAUL SIMON'S
GRACE-
LAND

THIS IS WHERE PEOPLE
WHO NEVER OTHERWISE
COME HERE, ENJOY
SITTING AND STARING
AT PEOPLE THEY
DON'T
KNOW

HEATE

20.20 STADSCHOUWBURG
THEATRE. A RETIRED
POLITICIAN PRESENTS HISTORY
NIGHT (BIT TOO AMICABLY)
A NEW DUTCH MOTTO IS
PROPOSED: "WHY NOT"
INSTEAD OF
JE MAINTIENDRAI
21.32 VAN REYBROUCK
WINS THE LIBRIS HISTORY
PRIZE FOR HIS BOOK
ON THE CONGO
(20.000 EUROS)

IRRITATING
BOUQUET

LOTS OF PEOPLE
WITH GREY
HAIR

TRAM
COMPANY
CAMERA'S

MESH

DAR
BLU

JOOP VAN DENENDE'S
THEATRE
DE LAMAR

OPENED RECENTLY
AFTER 5 YEARS OF
CONSTRUCTION. WON'T
THERE BE TOO MANY THEATRES
WHEN THEY ALL LOSE THEIR
SUBSIDIES? MAYBE WE SHOULD
TURN THE STADSCHOUWBURG
INTO A HISTORICAL
CULTURE MUSEUM?

PRONOUCE
IN THE FRENCH
MANNER:
AMERICAIN

HIS RESPONSE
IS IMPRESSIVE

AJAX BALCONY

STANI-
SLAVSKI
CAFÉ

TAX
SER
KIOS

ON 5-7 2009
ROB SITEK WAS BEATEN
HERE BY A TAXI DRIVER
AND DIED!
THREE DAYS LATER THIS
(MEMORIAL) KIOSK WAS
INSTALLED FOR THE SECURITY.
THIS MAN

RING
RING
RING

HOTEL
AMERICAN

BERMUDA TRIANGLE
(DANGEROUS TRAFFIC)

?

ALSO WORKED AS
SECURITY GUARD
AT THE HOUSE IN THE
BIG BROTHER TV SERIES
SO HE'S USED HANDLING
PEOPLE..

HE WORKS FOR
INTERNATIONA
SECURITY
AGENCY
(JUST ANOTHER
DUTCH
COMPANY)

ACTORS
WATERING HOLE

← RATHER
PONDEROUS
BUILDING

NEW
UNFRIENDLY
FOUNTAIN:
THE SIDES ARE
OFTEN WET DUE
TO THE WIND
(THE FISH ARE
SUPPOSEDLY
AN EARLY
PIECE BY
FORMER QUEEN
BEATRIX)

AROUND THE
CORNER CAFÉ THE
SMOESHAAN·
LAST ORDER CALL
AT 02:48

02.52 PSSSSST

GREY
CAB
TO BIJLMER
(SOUTH EAST)
FOR 15 EUROS
THAT'S CHEAP

LAST MONTH A
20 YEAR OLD FROM
AMSTERDAM WAS
PUSHED IN FRONT
OF A BUS!

AROUND
600 PEOPLE CATCH A
CAB AT LEIDSEPLEIN
BETWEEN 24.00 AND 04.00

03.20
TAXI QUEUE

SECRET

16

A WINCOR NIXDORF PROCASH ATM CAN HOLD 12.500 BANKNOTES. GIVEN THE CONSTANT QUEUES AT THE THREE ATMs THROUGHOUT THE NIGHT FROM 19.00 ON, THE MONEY BEING DISPENSED MUST RUN INTO HUNDREDS OF THOUSANDS!

Born and bred in the city, this is a square I try to avoid - or I go straight to where I need to be. While working on this drawing I did something I had never done before: I went into all the bars and spoke to people and allowed the place acquire a human quality.

KLM — OLD

RANDSTAD

BURGER KING

SIGN PROHIBITING 0% ALCOHOL

H&M

23.24 THE BURGER KING SECURITY GUARD IS A FEW TEETH SHORT. HE FOUGHT IN BOSNIA AND DID SOME STREET COACHING IN AMSTERDAM WEST. (SLOTERMEER) HE GETS AN ASSISTANT AT 3 O'CLOCK BECAUSE AFTER THAT EVERYBODY IS DRUNK.

6.5 METERS HIGH BEER GLASSES FILL WITH LIGHT (400 NEON TUBES)

HEINEKEN

HEINEKEN

ATM

IN THE QUEUE

PORTABLE URINALS (STINK)

WANDERING BIKES

EXTRA COLD! (RIDICULOUS)

...RATING ...ASE

OLD FASHIONED LAMPOST

INSIDE IS A MIXTURE OF SMOKE AND BEER

POLICE VAN STANDS HERE ON FRIDAY AND SATURDAY

...M 23.00 TO 06.00

PANCAKE HOUSE THEY DO PIZZAS TOO

BULLDOG WORLD COFFEESHOP

THE STAIRS ARE EXTRA STEEP WHEN DRUNK

TALL STAIRS TO THE MEMBERS ONLY CLUB "DE KRING" (THE CIRCLE)

THIS GUARD ACTUALLY LIVES IN SNEEK (FRIESLAND)

HEINEKEN CORNER

BAR REST. BLINQ

BIKES

TAXI

GABOR (AGE 24, WITH SPECS) FROM HUNGARY RENTS THIS RICKSHAW FOR 200 EURO'S A WEEK ON A GOOD NIGHT (FROM 22.00 TO 06.00) HE MAKES 150 EURO'S (LOTS OF RIDES TO THE RED LIGHT DISTRICT)

TOURISTS FOR TOURISTS

ART-HOUSE CINEMA

CITY

RANCHO RED MEAT

THEATRE RECENTLY THE BUILDING HAS BEEN RENOVATED TO ITS ORIGINAL SELF

03.20 GUYS REFUSED (ONLY REGULARS: BS)

THEY'RE MOROCCANS, BUT IS IT DISCRIMINATION?

MAYOR EBERHARD VAN DER LAAN PLANS TO DEPLOY UNDERCOVER OFFICERS TO FIND OUT... AND THEN?

ADVERT

TAXI

TAXI

TA...

TAXI

THIS IS THE ENTERTAINMENT AREA

PING

ADVERT

STANDING IN LINE FOR YOUR OWN MONEY

...CATED HERE

ATM

HOT DOG

PING

SAYS THE TRAM DRIVER

...02

...T'S GIVE AND ...AKE, SAYS THE HOTDOG STALLHOLDER ...'E'S A BUSINESSMAN AND ...HIS IS HIS SABBATICAL (REALLY!) ...LAIMS HIS NEW HOTDOG STALL ...S A PUSSY MAGNET!

THIS IS ABN-AMRO BANK OR WHAT'S LEFT OF IT LOOKS MORE LIKE A DESIGN FURNITURE STORE NOW

THE BALIE

HERE THE CULTURAL TYPES CONGREGATE FREE WI-FI

TAXIS QUEUEING UP

TONIGHT AT PARADISO KELIS (CURLY HAIR) OF: I HATE YOU SO MUCH AND MILKSHAKE FAME

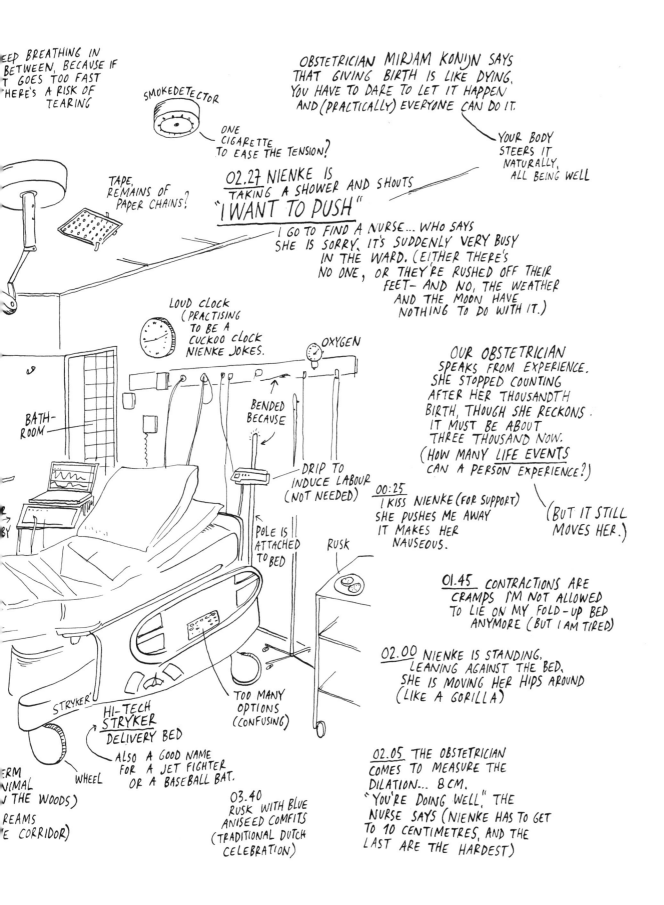

...EEP BREATHING IN BETWEEN, BECAUSE IF T GOES TOO FAST HERE'S A RISK OF TEARING

SMOKEDETECTOR

ONE CIGARETTE TO EASE THE TENSION?

OBSTETRICIAN MIRJAM KONIJN SAYS THAT GIVING BIRTH IS LIKE DYING. YOU HAVE TO DARE TO LET IT HAPPEN AND (PRACTICALLY) EVERYONE CAN DO IT.

YOUR BODY STEERS IT NATURALLY, ALL BEING WELL

TAPE, REMAINS OF PAPER CHAINS?

02.27 NIENKE IS TAKING A SHOWER AND SHOUTS "I WANT TO PUSH"

I GO TO FIND A NURSE... WHO SAYS SHE IS SORRY, IT'S SUDDENLY VERY BUSY IN THE WARD. (EITHER THERE'S NO ONE, OR THEY'RE RUSHED OFF THEIR FEET — AND NO, THE WEATHER AND THE MOON HAVE NOTHING TO DO WITH IT.)

LOUD CLOCK (PRACTISING TO BE A CUCKOO CLOCK NIENKE JOKES.

OXYGEN

OUR OBSTETRICIAN SPEAKS FROM EXPERIENCE. SHE STOPPED COUNTING AFTER HER THOUSANDTH BIRTH, THOUGH SHE RECKONS IT MUST BE ABOUT THREE THOUSAND NOW. (HOW MANY LIFE EVENTS CAN A PERSON EXPERIENCE?)

BATH-ROOM

BENDED BECAUSE

DRIP TO INDUCE LABOUR (NOT NEEDED)

POLE IS ATTACHED TO BED

00:25 I KISS NIENKE (FOR SUPPORT) SHE PUSHES ME AWAY IT MAKES HER NAUSEOUS.

(BUT IT STILL MOVES HER.)

RUSK

01.45 CONTRACTIONS ARE CRAMPS I'M NOT ALLOWED TO LIE ON MY FOLD-UP BED ANYMORE (BUT I AM TIRED)

02.00 NIENKE IS STANDING, LEANING AGAINST THE BED. SHE IS MOVING HER HIPS AROUND (LIKE A GORILLA)

STRYKER

HI-TECH STRYKER DELIVERY BED

ALSO A GOOD NAME FOR A JET FIGHTER OR A BASEBALL BAT.

WHEEL

TOO MANY OPTIONS (CONFUSING)

...RM ...IMAL ... THE WOODS)

...REAMS ...E CORRIDOR)

03.40 RUSK WITH BLUE ANISEED COMFITS (TRADITIONAL DUTCH CELEBRATION)

02.05 THE OBSTETRICIAN COMES TO MEASURE THE DILATION... 8 CM. "YOU'RE DOING WELL," THE NURSE SAYS (NIENKE HAS TO GET TO 10 CENTIMETRES, AND THE LAST ARE THE HARDEST)

ZAANSE SCHANS

OPEN-AIR HISTORICAL ATTRACTION (SINCE 1972)

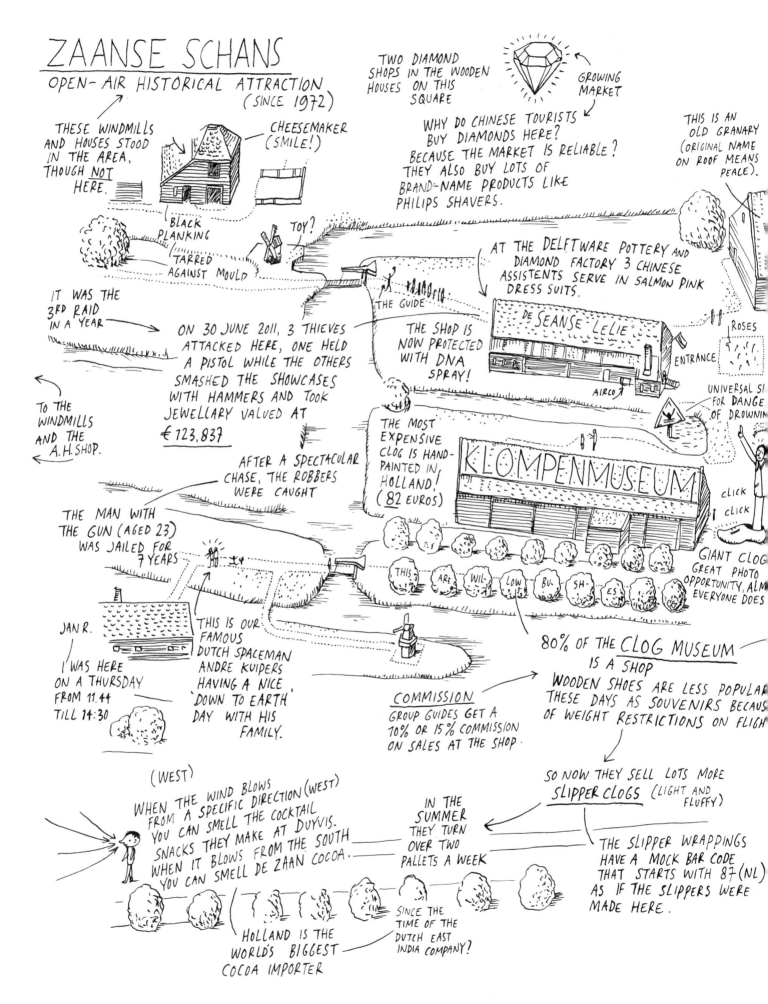

THESE WINDMILLS AND HOUSES STOOD IN THE AREA, THOUGH **NOT** HERE.

CHEESEMAKER (SMILE!)

BLACK PLANKING

TARRED AGAINST MOULD

TOY?

TWO DIAMOND SHOPS IN THE WOODEN HOUSES ON THIS SQUARE

GROWING MARKET

WHY DO CHINESE TOURISTS BUY DIAMONDS HERE? BECAUSE THE MARKET IS RELIABLE? THEY ALSO BUY LOTS OF BRAND-NAME PRODUCTS LIKE PHILIPS SHAVERS.

THIS IS AN OLD GRANARY (ORIGINAL NAME ON ROOF MEANS PEACE).

IT WAS THE 3RD RAID IN A YEAR

THE GUIDE

AT THE DELFTWARE POTTERY AND DIAMOND FACTORY 3 CHINESE ASSISTENTS SERVE IN SALMON PINK DRESS SUITS.

DE SEANSE LELIE

ROSES

ENTRANCE

AIRCO

ON 30 JUNE 2011, 3 THIEVES ATTACKED HERE, ONE HELD A PISTOL WHILE THE OTHERS SMASHED THE SHOWCASES WITH HAMMERS AND TOOK JEWELLARY VALUED AT € 123,837

THE SHOP IS NOW PROTECTED WITH DNA SPRAY!

UNIVERSAL SI FOR DANGE OF DROWNIN

TO THE WINDMILLS AND THE A.H. SHOP.

AFTER A SPECTACULAR CHASE, THE ROBBERS WERE CAUGHT

THE MOST EXPENSIVE CLOG IS HAND-PAINTED IN HOLLAND! (**82** EUROS)

KLOMPENMUSEUM

click click

THE MAN WITH THE GUN (AGED 23) WAS JAILED FOR 7 YEARS

GIANT CLOG GREAT PHOTO OPPORTUNITY. ALM EVERYONE DOES

THIS ARE WIL- LOW BU- SH- ES

JAN R.

I WAS HERE ON A THURSDAY FROM 11.44 TILL 14:30

THIS IS OUR FAMOUS DUTCH SPACEMAN ANDRE KUIPERS HAVING A NICE 'DOWN TO EARTH' DAY WITH HIS FAMILY.

COMMISSION GROUP GUIDES GET A 10% OR 15% COMMISSION ON SALES AT THE SHOP.

80% OF THE CLOG MUSEUM IS A SHOP WOODEN SHOES ARE LESS POPULAR THESE DAYS AS SOUVENIRS BECAUS OF WEIGHT RESTRICTIONS ON FLIGH

(WEST)

WHEN THE WIND BLOWS FROM A SPECIFIC DIRECTION (WEST) YOU CAN SMELL THE COCKTAIL SNACKS THEY MAKE AT DUYVIS. WHEN IT BLOWS FROM THE SOUTH YOU CAN SMELL DE ZAAN COCOA.

IN THE SUMMER THEY TURN OVER TWO PALLETS A WEEK

SO NOW THEY SELL LOTS MORE SLIPPER CLOGS (LIGHT AND FLUFFY)

THE SLIPPER WRAPPINGS HAVE A MOCK BAR CODE THAT STARTS WITH 87 (NL) AS IF THE SLIPPERS WERE MADE HERE.

HOLLAND IS THE WORLD'S BIGGEST COCOA IMPORTER

SINCE THE TIME OF THE DUTCH EAST INDIA COMPANY?

ZAANSE SCHANS

Location is everything. Even if it means moving a couple of windmills and those quaint wooden houses. Close by Amsterdam and Schiphol, Zaanse Schans is an ideal place for a daytrip and a bit of Dutch country air.

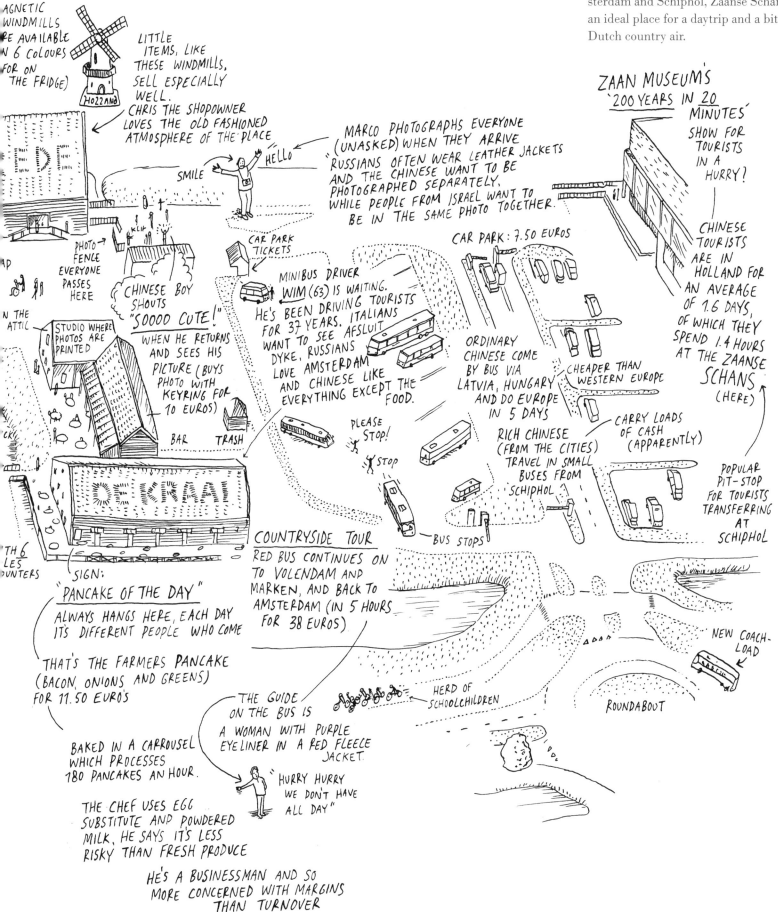

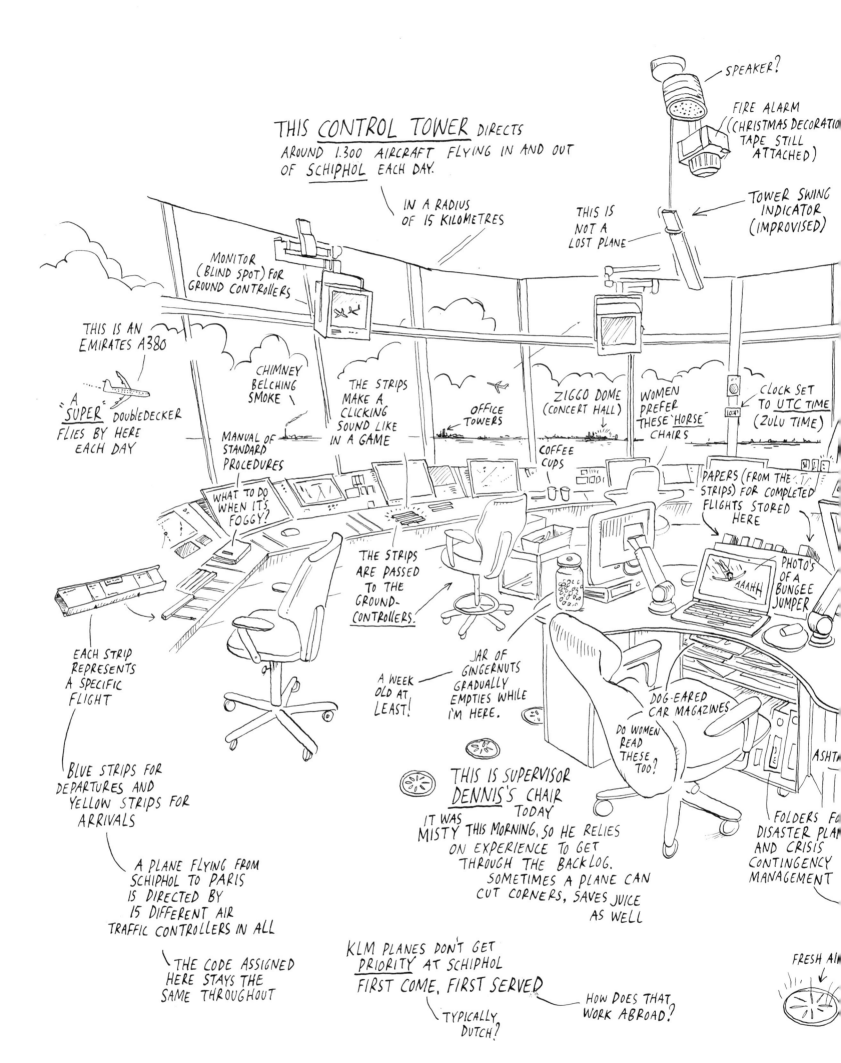

THIS **CONTROL TOWER** DIRECTS AROUND 1.300 AIRCRAFT FLYING IN AND OUT OF **SCHIPHOL** EACH DAY.

SPEAKER?

FIRE ALARM (CHRISTMAS DECORATION TAPE STILL ATTACHED)

IN A RADIUS OF 15 KILOMETRES

THIS IS NOT A LOST PLANE

TOWER SWING INDICATOR (IMPROVISED)

MONITOR (BLIND SPOT) FOR GROUND CONTROLLERS

THIS IS AN EMIRATES A380

"A **SUPER** DOUBLEDECKER FLIES BY HERE EACH DAY

CHIMNEY BELCHING SMOKE

THE STRIPS MAKE A CLICKING SOUND LIKE IN A GAME

OFFICE TOWERS

ZIGGO DOME (CONCERT HALL)

WOMEN PREFER THESE 'HORSE' CHAIRS

CLOCK SET TO UTC TIME (ZULU TIME)

MANUAL OF STANDARD PROCEDURES

WHAT TO DO WHEN IT'S FOGGY?

COFFEE CUPS

PAPERS (FROM THE STRIPS) FOR COMPLETED FLIGHTS STORED HERE

AAAHH

PHOTO'S OF A BUNGEE JUMPER

THE STRIPS ARE PASSED TO THE GROUND-CONTROLLERS.

JAR OF GINGERNUTS GRADUALLY EMPTIES WHILE I'M HERE.

A WEEK OLD AT LEAST!

DOG-EARED CAR MAGAZINES

EACH STRIP REPRESENTS A SPECIFIC FLIGHT

DO WOMEN READ THESE TOO?

ASHT

BLUE STRIPS FOR DEPARTURES AND YELLOW STRIPS FOR ARRIVALS

THIS IS SUPERVISOR **DENNIS'S** CHAIR TODAY
IT WAS MISTY THIS MORNING, SO HE RELIES ON EXPERIENCE TO GET THROUGH THE BACKLOG. SOMETIMES A PLANE CAN CUT CORNERS, SAVES JUICE AS WELL

FOLDERS FO DISASTER PLA AND CRISIS CONTINGENCY MANAGEMENT

A PLANE FLYING FROM SCHIPHOL TO PARIS IS DIRECTED BY 15 DIFFERENT AIR TRAFFIC CONTROLLERS IN ALL

THE CODE ASSIGNED HERE STAYS THE SAME THROUGHOUT

KLM PLANES DON'T GET **PRIORITY** AT SCHIPHOL FIRST COME, FIRST SERVED

FRESH AI

TYPICALLY DUTCH?

HOW DOES THAT WORK ABROAD?

From a distance of 15 kilometres, air traffic controllers are like modern gatekeepers piloting aircrafts safely into Amsterdam. Last year, some 52.6 million passengers passed through Schiphol, one of Europe's busiest airports.

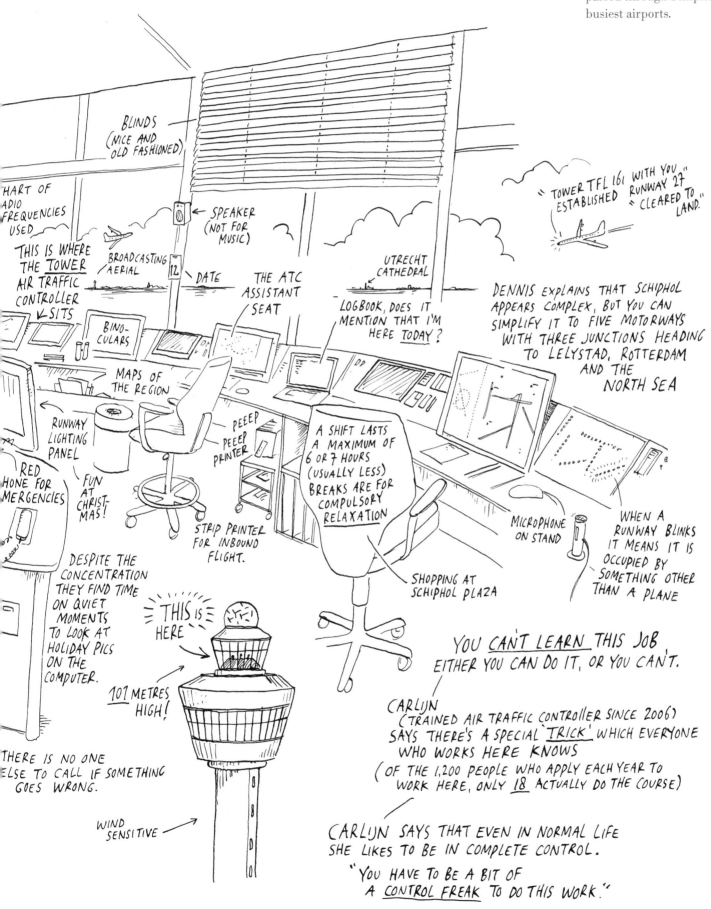

BLINDS
(NICE AND
OLD FASHIONED)

CHART OF
RADIO
FREQUENCIES
USED

SPEAKER
(NOT FOR
MUSIC)

THIS IS WHERE
THE TOWER
AIR TRAFFIC
CONTROLLER
SITS

BROADCASTING
AERIAL

DATE

THE ATC
ASSISTANT
SEAT

BINO-
CULARS

MAPS OF
THE REGION

UTRECHT
CATHEDRAL

LOGBOOK, DOES IT
MENTION THAT I'M
HERE TODAY?

" TOWER TFL 161 WITH YOU "
ESTABLISHED RUNWAY 27
" CLEARED TO
LAND."

DENNIS EXPLAINS THAT SCHIPHOL
APPEARS COMPLEX, BUT YOU CAN
SIMPLIFY IT TO FIVE MOTORWAYS
WITH THREE JUNCTIONS HEADING
TO LELYSTAD, ROTTERDAM
AND THE
NORTH SEA

RUNWAY
LIGHTING
PANEL

PEEEP
PEEEP
PRINTER

A SHIFT LASTS
A MAXIMUM OF
6 OR 7 HOURS
(USUALLY LESS)
BREAKS ARE FOR
COMPULSORY
RELAXATION

RED
PHONE FOR
EMERGENCIES

FUN
AT
CHRIST-
MAS!

STRIP PRINTER
FOR INBOUND
FLIGHT.

MICROPHONE
ON STAND

WHEN A
RUNWAY BLINKS
IT MEANS IT IS
OCCUPIED BY
SOMETHING OTHER
THAN A PLANE

SHOPPING AT
SCHIPHOL PLAZA

DESPITE THE
CONCENTRATION
THEY FIND TIME
ON QUIET
MOMENTS
TO LOOK AT
HOLIDAY PICS
ON THE
COMPUTER.

THIS IS
HERE

YOU CAN'T LEARN THIS JOB
EITHER YOU CAN DO IT, OR YOU CAN'T.

CARLIJN
(TRAINED AIR TRAFFIC CONTROLLER SINCE 2006)
SAYS THERE'S A SPECIAL 'TRICK' WHICH EVERYONE
WHO WORKS HERE KNOWS
(OF THE 1,200 PEOPLE WHO APPLY EACH YEAR TO
WORK HERE, ONLY 18 ACTUALLY DO THE COURSE)

101 METRES
HIGH!

THERE IS NO ONE
ELSE TO CALL IF SOMETHING
GOES WRONG.

WIND
SENSITIVE

CARLIJN SAYS THAT EVEN IN NORMAL LIFE
SHE LIKES TO BE IN COMPLETE CONTROL.

"YOU HAVE TO BE A BIT OF
A CONTROL FREAK TO DO THIS WORK."

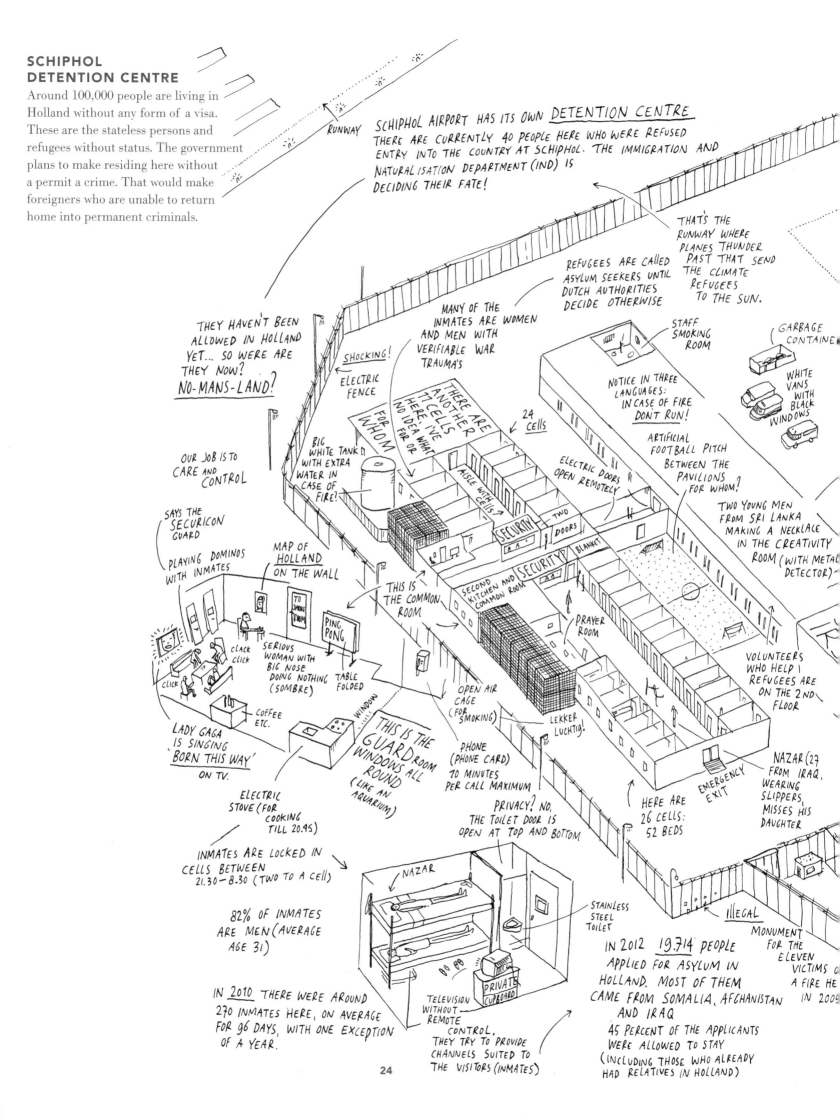

SCHIPHOL DETENTION CENTRE

Around 100,000 people are living in Holland without any form of a visa. These are the stateless persons and refugees without status. The government plans to make residing here without a permit a crime. That would make foreigners who are unable to return home into permanent criminals.

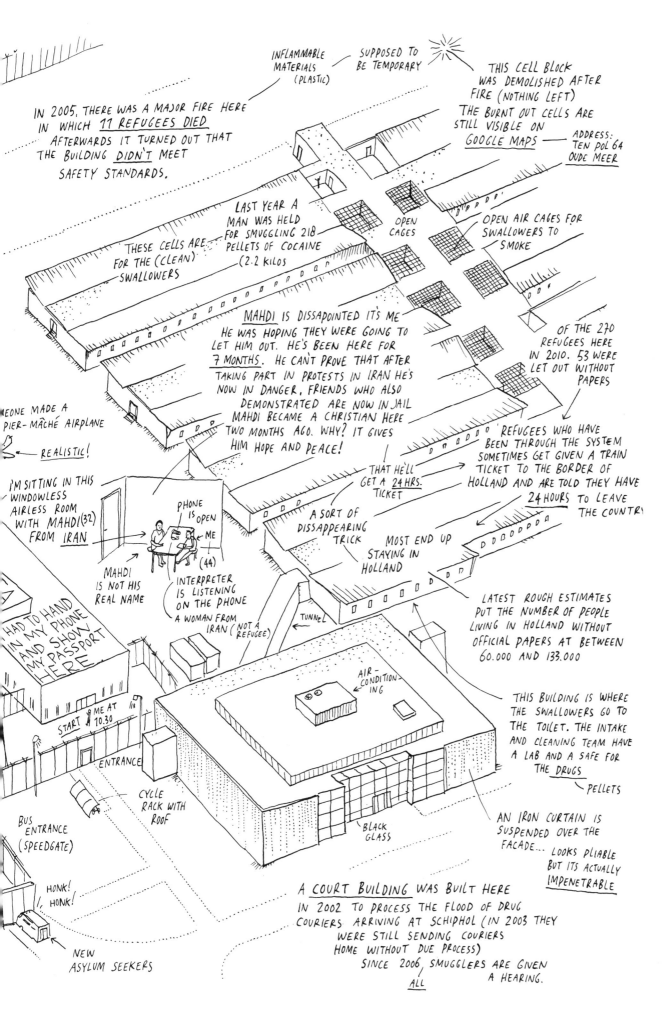

INFLAMMABLE MATERIALS (PLASTIC) — SUPPOSED TO BE TEMPORARY

IN 2005, THERE WAS A MAJOR FIRE HERE IN WHICH 11 REFUGEES DIED AFTERWARDS IT TURNED OUT THAT THE BUILDING DIDN'T MEET SAFETY STANDARDS.

THIS CELL BLOCK WAS DEMOLISHED AFTER FIRE (NOTHING LEFT) THE BURNT OUT CELLS ARE STILL VISIBLE ON GOOGLE MAPS — ADDRESS: TEN POL 64 OUDE MEER

THESE CELLS ARE FOR THE (CLEAN) SWALLOWERS

LAST YEAR A MAN WAS HELD FOR SMUGGLING 218 PELLETS OF COCAINE (2.2 KILOS

OPEN CAGES

OPEN AIR CAGES FOR SWALLOWERS TO SMOKE

OF THE 270 REFUGEES HERE IN 2010. 53 WERE LET OUT WITHOUT PAPERS

MAHDI IS DISSAPOINTED IT'S ME HE WAS HOPING THEY WERE GOING TO LET HIM OUT. HE'S BEEN HERE FOR 7 MONTHS. HE CAN'T PROVE THAT AFTER TAKING PART IN PROTESTS IN IRAN HE'S NOW IN DANGER. FRIENDS WHO ALSO DEMONSTRATED ARE NOW IN JAIL MAHDI BECAME A CHRISTIAN HERE TWO MONTHS AGO. WHY? IT GIVES HIM HOPE AND PEACE!

EONE MADE A PIER-MÂCHÉ AIRPLANE — REALISTIC!

I'M SITTING IN THIS WINDOWLESS AIRLESS ROOM WITH MAHDI (32) FROM IRAN

PHONE IS OPEN — ME — (44)

MAHDI IS NOT HIS REAL NAME

INTERPRETER IS LISTENING ON THE PHONE — A WOMAN FROM IRAN (NOT A REFUGEE)

THAT HE'LL GET A 24 HRS. TICKET

A SORT OF DISSAPPEARING TRICK

TUNNEL

REFUGEES WHO HAVE BEEN THROUGH THE SYSTEM SOMETIMES GET GIVEN A TRAIN TICKET TO THE BORDER OF HOLLAND AND ARE TOLD THEY HAVE 24 HOURS TO LEAVE THE COUNTRY

MOST END UP STAYING IN HOLLAND

LATEST ROUGH ESTIMATES PUT THE NUMBER OF PEOPLE LIVING IN HOLLAND WITHOUT OFFICIAL PAPERS AT BETWEEN 60.000 AND 133.000

HAD TO HAND IN MY PHONE AND SHOW MY PASSPORT HERE

START ME AT 10.30

ENTRANCE

CYCLE RACK WITH ROOF

AIR-CONDITION-ING

THIS BUILDING IS WHERE THE SWALLOWERS GO TO THE TOILET. THE INTAKE AND CLEANING TEAM HAVE A LAB AND A SAFE FOR THE DRUGS — PELLETS

BUS ENTRANCE (SPEEDGATE)

BLACK GLASS

AN IRON CURTAIN IS SUSPENDED OVER THE FACADE... LOOKS PLIABLE BUT ITS ACTUALLY IMPENETRABLE

HONK! HONK!

NEW ASYLUM SEEKERS

A COURT BUILDING WAS BUILT HERE IN 2002 TO PROCESS THE FLOOD OF DRUG COURIERS ARRIVING AT SCHIPHOL (IN 2003 THEY WERE STILL SENDING COURIERS HOME WITHOUT DUE PROCESS) SINCE 2006, SMUGGLERS ARE GIVEN ALL A HEARING.

INV
TIV

EN-
VE

Amsterdam took root and grew in this marshy land-scape because it was an ideal place to make money. Opportunism and pride still make Amsterdam complacent and progressive to this day.

IN THIS BUILDING ON AMSTERDAM'S PRINS HENDRIKKADE YOUTH CENTRE **FANTASIO**

USED TO ATTRACT CROWDS OF YOUNG PEOPLE FROM AROUND THE WORLD IN 1968 AND 1969

SEVENTEEN MONTHS ON, FANTASIO'S STAFF DECIDED IT WAS TIME FOR A CHANGE, AND POSTED THIS NOTICE ON THE WALL

I WAS ONE YEAR (
THERE WERE
LIVING IN A
WITH ONE
ANY SURINAME

WALLPAPER

(TO AIR YOUR FEELINGS AND THOUGHTS)

FANTASIO IN IT'S CURRENT FORM IS NO LONGER viable because the way things are is no good! everything is crushed dead by the crowd. FANTASIO has become a big COMMERCIAL business. We don't know how we're going to change things yet. You can come round to the office or write on the paper here....

AFTER THE CHAOS AT FANTASIO IT WAS TIME TO CONCENTRATE AT THE KOSMOS MEDITATION CENTRE. SINCE 2012 AN INTERNATIONAL ART CENTRE (WHICH EXPLAINS THE ENGLISH TITLE)

de App

FANTASIO WAS THE FIRST PLACE WHERE PEOPLE COULD BUY AND SMOKE POT (OFFICIALLY TOLERATED)

25 YEARS LATER (IN 1995) THERE WERE 1.450 COFFEESHOPS IN HOLLAND
(I.E SOFT DRUGS)

SINCE THEN THE MUNICIPAL POLICY HAS BEEN TO REDUCE THE NUMBER, SO IN 2013 THERE ARE 650 LEFT.

THIS WAS HERE IN 1969

APPEL

LOW-HANGING LAMPS OVER CARPET COVERED PALLETS FOR HANGING OUT.
LATER THEY CALLED IT LOUNGING!

CONDOM DISPENSER

CONTRACEPTION WASN'T LEGALISED UNTIL 1969
THE SEXUAL REVOLUTION!

TEA AND SPACE CAKE

HOTPANTS
SUPER
BERLA
SENT
WEARIN
MA
(WH
?

FANTASIO

Today's Amsterdam had its formative years in the late 1960s. Liberal Dutch attitudes to recreational drugs and sexual promiscuity were first nurtured in this building on Prins Hendrik Kade.

1969
NY PEOPLE
RDAM THEN AS NOW,
FERENCE: HARDLY
RKS OR MOROCCANS

AMSTERDAM WAS
A GREY CITY)

THE FRONT OF THE BUILDING IS MORE ROBUST

LOTS OF APPEL WOMEN ARE WORKING ON (WHITE) APPLES HERE IN THE ATTIC

IMPRESSIVE! IN 1968

LIQUID SLIDES WITH ECOLINE BLUB BLUB

FILM PROJECTOR

DAYLIGHT

PAINTER

IN 1966, AMSTERDAM'S NARCOTICS BRIGADE EXPANDED FROM 2 MEN TO 6!

ANN DE MEESTER (DIRECTOR) CHECKING EMAILS

ts centre

PORTRAIT OF LENIN, JOKE? BLA BLA BLA

NOTHING WAS WRITTEN ON PAPER (SMART MOVE)

DANSEN

BALCONY

OOOH

IN 1968, DISCUSSIONS WERE HELD WITH THE MUNICIPALITY AND THE RESULT WAS TODAY'S TOLERATION POLICY. THEY THOUGHT THAT POT SMOKERS WOULD REMAIN A SMALL GROUP

DANCER AIMEE MARS (ART MAKES YOU STRONG)

OOIKOOI RESTAURANT (RICE WITH MUSH AND VEG)

HEALTHY!

ROPE ON BALCONY TO ESCAPE IN CASE OF FIRE

I (JAN R.) DREW A 9 METRE HIGH DRAWING ON THIS WALL ABOUT FANTASIO, WHICH IS PART OF THE ARTIFICIAL AMSTERDAM EXHIBITION. IT OPENED THE 29TH OF JUNE 2013 (LOTS OF PEOPLE SHOWED UP FROM SIXTIES)

BUY? NO, SWAP!

FRANK

NO CHANGE

ONLY IDEALS!

PALLET

REQUIRED BY THE FIRE BRIGADE

MOES

STAURANT 2013

ENTRANCE

JAZZ CELLAR LIVE MUSIC EVERY FRIDAY NIGHT

THIS WAS THE DIGGER SHOP (SWAP SHOP) IN THE TEAHOUSE IMITATING RADICAL ANARCHIST ARTISTS IN SAN FRANCISCO

HIPPIES WHO WANTED A WORLD WITHOUT MONEY

1968
EUM SCHOOL IN AMSTERDAM
L HOME (JUNE 2013) FOR
PANTS, BECAUSE IT MIGHT
CHERS FEEL UNCOMFORTABLE!
SPONSIBLE FOR WHOM?)

DEBATE NIGHTS ON SATURDAY ABOUT SUBJECTS LIKE ADDICTION

BUCKETS OF SAND FOR SICK (HEROIN SIDE EFFECT)

NOT A LOT WAS KNOWN ABOUT IT IN 1969

NOW ON INTERNET THERE'S LOADS OF SWAP SITES ALTHOUGH THEY AREN'T ANARCHIST AT ALL!

LIKE: ZILCH.COM
SWAPATYOUROWNRISK.COM

THIS IS PERHAPS THE MOST MODERN AND CERTAINLY THE MOST PROGRESSIVE FACILITY IN AMSTERDAM

THE PEOPLE ON THE OTHER SIDE OF THE WINDOW AREN'T CALLED JUNKS OR USERS AT THIS SOUTHEAST AMSTERDAM CLINIC, EVEN IF THAT'S WHAT THEY ARE! NO, HERE THE PEOPLE WHO COME TO GET HEROIN OR METHADON ARE CALLED PATIENT

DELEGATIONS FROM ABROAD VISIT REGULARLY.

WHITE LIGHT.

WOODEN PANELS

THIS IS THE ORDINARY MEDICIN CABINET

WOODEN PANEL

CONCRETE

METHADONE COUNTER.
THEY HAVE TO DRINK IT STRAIGHT AWAY AND THE WOMAN WHO SITS HERE MAKES SURE.

SHORT HAIR RED RIMMED GLASSES, BRIGHT CHEERFUL

POSTER

REPORT VIOLENCE

SMILE!

THIS IS THE NEEDLE ROOM.
THEY HAVE TO CLEAN IT THEMSELVES AFTER USE THERE'S PLASTER AND BANDAGES (ONE AT A TIME)

MIRROR TO CHECK

SCREEN SHOWS WHAT EACH PATIENT GETS
(DOSE)

OFFICE HUMOUR

PLASTIC CUPS

FLUID

LOCK

INDICATOR MEASURES THE AMOUNT

WINDOW COVERED WITH PLASTIC

DRAWING OF A CAKE.
SOMEONE SAID THEY WANTED A CAKE, SO SOMEONE ELSE DREW ONE HA HA HA

THEY'RE AL- WAYS CON- VINCED ITS TOO LITTLE (PARA- NOIA)

TUBE THROUGH WALL

OLD-SCHOOL BIN

PLASTIC SUPER- MARKET BAG NO IDEA WHAT'S IN IT.

AFTER USING, THE PATIENT THROWS THE NEEDLE INTO THE TUBE THAT LEADS TO A BUCKET

WORKING WOMEN (SEX WO GET 12 CONDOM A DAY (THE MEN ONLY GET ONE) NOT THE BEST TH THEY GET GL APPROVED BY (ONE SIZE F

THE PHARMACEUTICAL HEROIN
IS BROUGHT HERE IN A DARK- BLUE SECURITY TRANSPORT VAN (WITH MOTORISED ESCORT)

WHO MANUFACTURES IT IS SECRET

IT'S NOT FROM THE STREET

AROUND 110 KILO IS REQUIRED ANNUALLY TO SUPPLY 300 PATIENTS
(THE HEROIN IS NOT KEPT HERE!)

THIS IS A METHADONE TAP (NOT A BEER TAP) THE ADJACENT BOTTLE CONTAINS FLUID.
METHADONE DOESN'T WORK AS AN ALTERNATIVE FOR EVERYONE. IT DOESN'T HAVE THE SAME RUSH AS HEROINE. (APPARENTLY IT'S FOUL, TASTES LIKE VANILLA)

SOME PATIENTS TAKE UP TO 220 ML WHILE 30 ML WOULD KNOCK A NORMAL HEALTHY PERSON OUT.

THE WOMAN WHO WORKS HERE SAYS SHE ENJOYS HER JOB VERY VERY MUCH!
(THEY'RE RECRUITING...)

HEROIN CLINIC

When heroin arrived in the 1960s, it was cheaper than hashish, speed or opium. A decade passed and by 1980 there were over 10,000 heroin addicts in Amsterdam. Today, a shrinking clique of aging users remains.

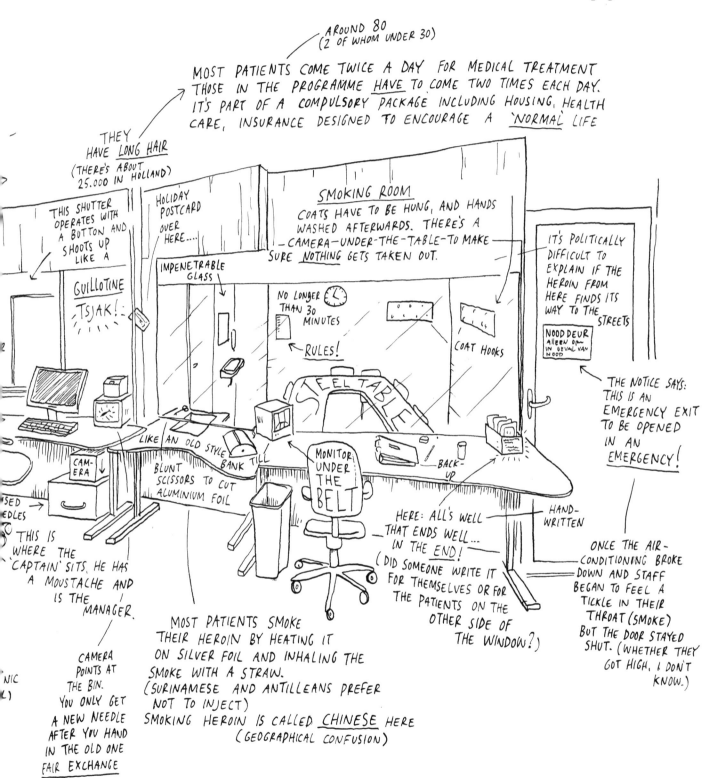

AROUND 80
(2 OF WHOM UNDER 30)

MOST PATIENTS COME TWICE A DAY FOR MEDICAL TREATMENT
THOSE IN THE PROGRAMME HAVE TO COME TWO TIMES EACH DAY.
IT'S PART OF A COMPULSORY PACKAGE INCLUDING HOUSING, HEALTH
CARE, INSURANCE DESIGNED TO ENCOURAGE A 'NORMAL' LIFE

THEY HAVE LONG HAIR
(THERE'S ABOUT 25.000 IN HOLLAND)

THIS SHUTTER OPERATES WITH A BUTTON AND SHOOTS UP LIKE A

GUILLOTINE
TSJAK!

HOLIDAY POSTCARD OVER HERE....

IMPENETRABLE GLASS

SMOKING ROOM
COATS HAVE TO BE HUNG, AND HANDS
WASHED AFTERWARDS. THERE'S A
—CAMERA—UNDER-THE-TABLE-TO-MAKE—
SURE NOTHING GETS TAKEN OUT.

IT'S POLITICALLY DIFFICULT TO EXPLAIN IF THE HEROIN FROM HERE FINDS ITS WAY TO THE STREETS

NO LONGER THAN 30 MINUTES

←RULES!

STEEL TABLE

COAT HOOKS

NOOD DEUR
ALLEEN OPEN
IN GEVAL VAN
NOOD

THE NOTICE SAYS:
THIS IS AN EMERGENCY EXIT TO BE OPENED IN AN EMERGENCY!

CAM-ERA

LIKE AN OLD STYLE BANK TILL

BLUNT SCISSORS TO CUT ALUMINIUM FOIL

MONITOR UNDER THE BELT

BACK-UP

HAND-WRITTEN

SED EDLES

THIS IS WHERE THE 'CAPTAIN' SITS. HE HAS A MOUSTACHE AND IS THE MANAGER.

HERE: ALL'S WELL THAT ENDS WELL... IN THE END!
(DID SOMEONE WRITE IT FOR THEMSELVES OR FOR THE PATIENTS ON THE OTHER SIDE OF THE WINDOW?)

ONCE THE AIR-CONDITIONING BROKE DOWN AND STAFF BEGAN TO FEEL A TICKLE IN THEIR THROAT (SMOKE) BUT THE DOOR STAYED SHUT. (WHETHER THEY GOT HIGH, I DON'T KNOW.)

NIC)

CAMERA POINTS AT THE BIN.
YOU ONLY GET A NEW NEEDLE AFTER YOU HAND IN THE OLD ONE
FAIR EXCHANGE

MOST PATIENTS SMOKE THEIR HEROIN BY HEATING IT ON SILVER FOIL AND INHALING THE SMOKE WITH A STRAW.
(SURINAMESE AND ANTILLEANS PREFER NOT TO INJECT)
SMOKING HEROIN IS CALLED CHINESE HERE
(GEOGRAPHICAL CONFUSION)

I WAS HERE FROM 14.15 TO 16.40

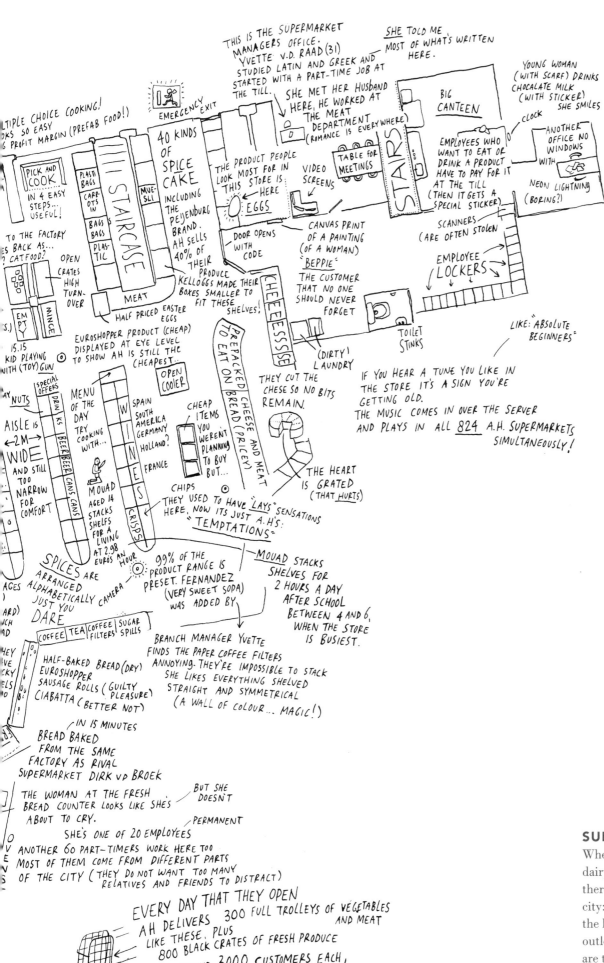

SUPERMARKET

When I was a boy, I used to pass three dairy shops on my way to school. Now there are practically none left anywhere in city: instead there are supermarkets, like the huge Albert Heijn chain. They had 34 outlets in Amsterdam in 1975; today there are twice that number.

MIRROR

WOODEN FRAME

THIS WINDOW NO LONGER OPENS

IS THE ROMANCE OF NEON LIGHTING A CULTURAL THING?

MEN ONLY!
(NO NOTICE THOUGH)

THIS MINI BARBERSHOP IS IN THE BASEMENT OF EKMEL, TURKISH STUDY CENTRE

IN SLOTERVAART AMSTERDAM

CROCHET THINGY

BASKET WIT FOLDED PLAS BAGS

WAX

WITH CLASSROOMS, DORMITORIES (FOR 80 BOYS) AND A PRAYER ROOM.

EXT TOW

A KIND OF BOARDINGSCHOOL BUT FOR ORDINARY CHILDREN

ABZEHK: EXTRA STRONG WAX

AHMED (38) WEARS SLIPPERS HE DOESN'T KNOW ANY DIFFICULT HAIRSTYLES, THOUGH HE CAN TELL WHO'LL BE A DIFFICULT CUSTOMER BEFORE THEY SIT DOWN.

TWEEZER AND SPIRAL FOR FACIAL HAIR.

STUDENTS PAY 5 EURO'S FOR A HAIRCUT. THEY MISS OUT ON THE POPULAR HAIRCUTS (SO NO LAYERED STYLE.)

HAIR GOES FROM FLOOR TO

CIRCULATION 20.000

LOCALS (AND ME) PAY 10 EURO'S

CHAIR FOR FRIENDS WHO CONSTANTLY POP IN FOR A CHAT.

EACH TIME SOMEONE E

SMELLS
- OF FRIED FOOD FROM THE TURKISH SNACK-BAR NEXT DOOR

ARE THESE TOWELS USED?

HEADREST DOESN'T GO UP.

SPECIALTY:

"BARBERSHOP"

CHIPS/DONER/SALAD WITH CHEESE ON TOP MELTED UNDER THE GRILL.

HAIRLINE TEAR ORANGE FAUX LEATHER

'A LITTLE SHORTER?' AHMED ASKS AS I SIT IN THE CHAIR. I NOD AND TRY TO SEE THE CLOCK IN THE MIRROR SO I CAN TIME HOW LONG IT TAKES (23 MINUTES)

GENUINE ROTTERDAM COMBINATION

FOR THE CONNOISSEURS!

MY GIRLFRIEND WONDERS WHAT HAPPENED WHEN I GET HOME (MY HAIR IS LOOKING PRETTY GOOD AGAIN TODAY)

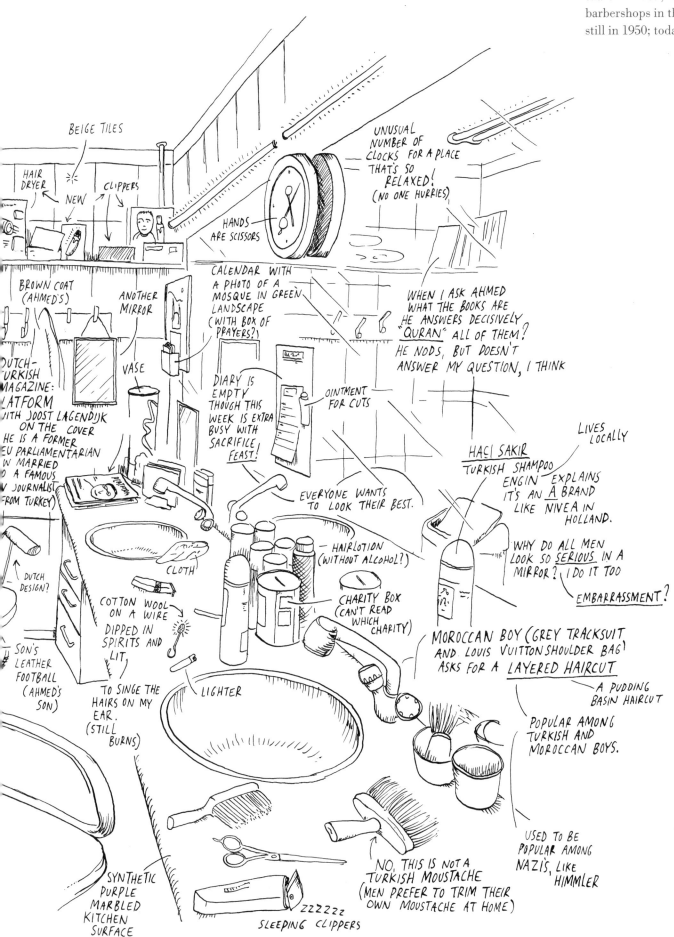

BEIGE TILES

HAIR DRYER

NEW

CLIPPERS

HANDS ARE SCISSORS

UNUSUAL NUMBER OF CLOCKS FOR A PLACE THAT'S SO RELAXED! (NO ONE HURRIES)

BROWN COAT (AHMED'S)

ANOTHER MIRROR

VASE

CALENDAR WITH A PHOTO OF A MOSQUE IN GREEN LANDSCAPE (WITH BOX OF PRAYERS?)

WHEN I ASK AHMED WHAT THE BOOKS ARE HE ANSWERS DECISIVELY "QURAN" ALL OF THEM? HE NODS, BUT DOESN'T ANSWER MY QUESTION, I THINK

DUTCH-TURKISH MAGAZINE: PLATFORM WITH JOOST LAGENDIJK ON THE COVER (HE IS A FORMER EU PARLIAMENTARIAN NOW MARRIED TO A FAMOUS TV JOURNALIST FROM TURKEY)

DIARY IS EMPTY THOUGH THIS WEEK IS EXTRA BUSY WITH SACRIFICE FEAST!

OINTMENT FOR CUTS

HACI SAKIR TURKISH SHAMPOO ENGIN EXPLAINS IT'S AN A BRAND LIKE NIVEA IN HOLLAND.

LIVES LOCALLY

DUTCH DESIGN?

CLOTH

EVERYONE WANTS TO LOOK THEIR BEST.

HAIRLOTION (WITHOUT ALCOHOL?)

WHY DO ALL MEN LOOK SO SERIOUS IN A MIRROR? I DO IT TOO

EMBARRASSMENT?

COTTON WOOL ON A WIRE DIPPED IN SPIRITS AND LIT.

CHARITY BOX (CAN'T READ WHICH CHARITY)

MOROCCAN BOY (GREY TRACKSUIT AND LOUIS VUITTON SHOULDER BAG) ASKS FOR A LAYERED HAIRCUT

A PUDDING BASIN HAIRCUT

SON'S LEATHER FOOTBALL (AHMED'S SON)

TO SINGE THE HAIRS ON MY EAR. (STILL BURNS)

LIGHTER

POPULAR AMONG TURKISH AND MOROCCAN BOYS.

SYNTHETIC PURPLE MARBLED KITCHEN SURFACE

NO, THIS IS NOT A TURKISH MOUSTACHE (MEN PREFER TO TRIM THEIR OWN MOUSTACHE AT HOME)

USED TO BE POPULAR AMONG NAZIS, LIKE HIMMLER

ZZZZZZ SLEEPING CLIPPERS

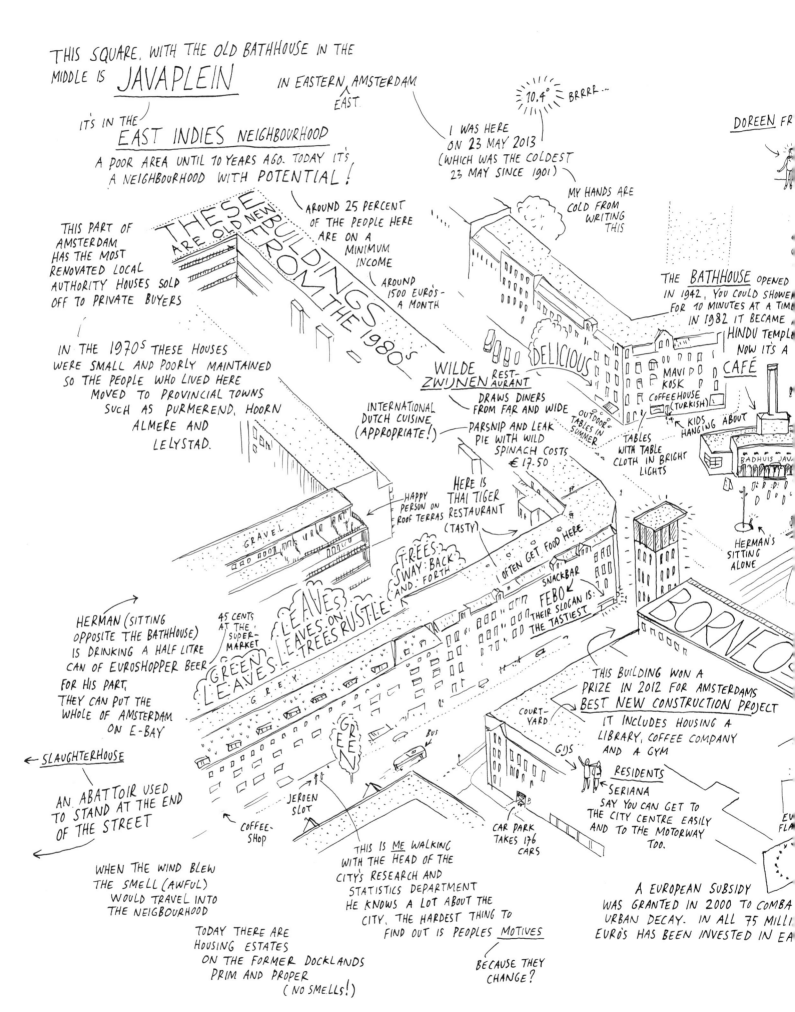

THIS SQUARE, WITH THE OLD BATHHOUSE IN THE MIDDLE IS **JAVAPLEIN** IN EASTERN, AMSTERDAM EAST.

IT'S IN THE EAST INDIES NEIGHBOURHOOD

A POOR AREA UNTIL 10 YEARS AGO. TODAY IT'S A NEIGHBOURHOOD WITH POTENTIAL!

10.4° BRRRR...

I WAS HERE ON 23 MAY 2013 (WHICH WAS THE COLDEST 23 MAY SINCE 1901)

MY HANDS ARE COLD FROM WRITING THIS

DOREEN FR...

THIS PART OF AMSTERDAM HAS THE MOST RENOVATED LOCAL AUTHORITY HOUSES SOLD OFF TO PRIVATE BUYERS

THESE ARE OLD NEW BUILDINGS FROM THE 1980s

AROUND 25 PERCENT OF THE PEOPLE HERE ARE ON A MINIMUM INCOME

AROUND 1500 EURO'S A MONTH

THE BATHHOUSE OPENED IN 1942, YOU COULD SHOWER FOR 10 MINUTES AT A TIME IN 1982 IT BECAME A HINDU TEMPLE NOW IT'S A CAFÉ

IN THE 1970s THESE HOUSES WERE SMALL AND POORLY MAINTAINED SO THE PEOPLE WHO LIVED HERE MOVED TO PROVINCIAL TOWNS SUCH AS PURMEREND, HOORN ALMERE AND LELYSTAD.

WILDE ZWIJNEN REST-AURANT

DELICIOUS

MAVI KOSK COFFEEHOUSE (TURKISH)

KIDS HANGING ABOUT

INTERNATIONAL DUTCH CUISINE (APPROPRIATE!)

DRAWS DINERS FROM FAR AND WIDE

OUTDOOR TABLES IN SUMMER

TABLES WITH TABLE CLOTH IN BRIGHT LIGHTS

BADHUIS JAV...

PARSNIP AND LEAK PIE WITH WILD SPINACH COSTS €17.50

HERE IS THAI TIGER RESTAURANT (TASTY)

HAPPY PERSON ON ROOF TERRAS

GRAVEL

I OFTEN GET FOOD HERE

HERMAN'S SITTING ALONE

TREES SWAY BACK AND FORTH

LEAVES LEAVES ON TREES RUSTLE. GREEN LEAVES. LEAVES. G.R.E.X.

SNACKBAR FEBO THEIR SLOGAN IS: THE TASTIEST

BORNEO...

HERMAN (SITTING OPPOSITE THE BATHHOUSE) IS DRINKING A HALF LITRE CAN OF EUROSHOPPER BEER FOR HIS PART, THEY CAN PUT THE WHOLE OF AMSTERDAM ON E-BAY

45 CENTS AT THE SUPER-MARKET

GREEN

THIS BUILDING WON A PRIZE IN 2012 FOR AMSTERDAMS BEST NEW CONSTRUCTION PROJECT

IT INCLUDES HOUSING A LIBRARY, COFFEE COMPANY AND A GYM

COURT-YARD

GIJS

RESIDENTS

SERIANA SAY YOU CAN GET TO THE CITY CENTRE EASILY AND TO THE MOTORWAY TOO.

EU... FLA...

SLAUGHTERHOUSE

AN ABATTOIR USED TO STAND AT THE END OF THE STREET

JEROEN SLOT

COFFEE-SHOP

BUS

CAR PARK TAKES 176 CARS

WHEN THE WIND BLEW THE SMELL (AWFUL) WOULD TRAVEL INTO THE NEIGBOURHOOD

THIS IS ME WALKING WITH THE HEAD OF THE CITY'S RESEARCH AND STATISTICS DEPARTMENT HE KNOWS A LOT ABOUT THE CITY, THE HARDEST THING TO FIND OUT IS PEOPLES MOTIVES

TODAY THERE ARE HOUSING ESTATES ON THE FORMER DOCKLANDS PRIM AND PROPER (NO SMELLS!)

BECAUSE THEY CHANGE?

A EUROPEAN SUBSIDY WAS GRANTED IN 2000 TO COMBA... URBAN DECAY. IN ALL 75 MILLI... EURO'S HAS BEEN INVESTED IN EA...

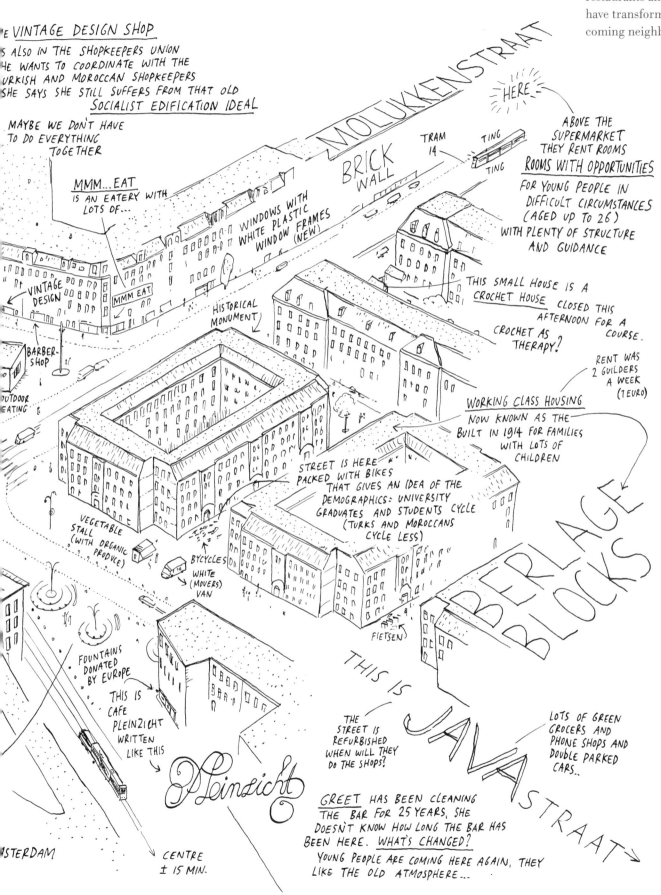

JAVAPLEIN

More subsidised rented homes were sold to tenants in this part of the city than anywhere else. A major hotel, trendy restaurants and Mediterranean fountains have transformed Javaplein into an up-coming neighbourhood.

E VINTAGE DESIGN SHOP
S ALSO IN THE SHOPKEEPERS UNION
HE WANTS TO COORDINATE WITH THE
URKISH AND MOROCCAN SHOPKEEPERS
SHE SAYS SHE STILL SUFFERS FROM THAT OLD
SOCIALIST EDIFICATION IDEAL

MAYBE WE DON'T HAVE
TO DO EVERYTHING
TOGETHER

MMM...EAT
IS AN EATERY WITH
LOTS OF...

WINDOWS WITH
WHITE PLASTIC
WINDOW FRAMES
(NEW)

MOLUKKENSTRAAT

HERE

BRICK WALL

TRAM 14

TING
TING

ABOVE THE
SUPERMARKET
THEY RENT ROOMS
ROOMS WITH OPPORTUNITIES
FOR YOUNG PEOPLE IN
DIFFICULT CIRCUMSTANCES
(AGED UP TO 26)
WITH PLENTY OF STRUCTURE
AND GUIDANCE

THIS SMALL HOUSE IS A
CROCHET HOUSE CLOSED THIS
AFTERNOON FOR A
CROCHET AS COURSE.
THERAPY?

VINTAGE
DESIGN

MMM EAT

BARBER-
SHOP

OUTDOOR
EATING

HISTORICAL
MONUMENT

RENT WAS
2 GUILDERS
A WEEK
(1 EURO)

WORKING CLASS HOUSING
NOW KNOWN AS THE
BUILT IN 1914 FOR FAMILIES
WITH LOTS OF
CHILDREN

STREET IS HERE
PACKED WITH BIKES
THAT GIVES AN IDEA OF THE
DEMOGRAPHICS: UNIVERSITY
GRADUATES AND STUDENTS CYCLE
(TURKS AND MOROCCANS
CYCLE LESS)

VEGETABLE
STALL
(WITH ORGANIC
PRODUCE)

BYCYCLES
WHITE
(MOVERS)
VAN

FIETSEN

BERLAGE
BLOCKS

FOUNTAINS
DONATED
BY EUROPE

THIS IS
CAFE
PLEINZICHT
WRITTEN
LIKE THIS

Pleinzicht

THE
STREET IS
REFURBISHED
WHEN WILL THEY
DO THE SHOPS?

THIS IS JAVASTRAAT

LOTS OF GREEN
GROCERS AND
PHONE SHOPS AND
DOUBLE PARKED
CARS..

STERDAM

CENTRE
± 15 MIN.

GREET HAS BEEN CLEANING
THE BAR FOR 25 YEARS, SHE
DOESN'T KNOW HOW LONG THE BAR HAS
BEEN HERE. WHAT'S CHANGED?
YOUNG PEOPLE ARE COMING HERE AGAIN, THEY
LIKE THE OLD ATMOSPHERE...

THIS IS ONE OF FOUR KITCHENS AT <u>VREDENBURGH</u> COMMUNE AT THE END OF OUDE ZIJDSVOORBURGWAL IN THE CENTRE OF AMSTERDAM

THERE ARE THREE GROUPS LIVING HERE, COMPRISING 17 PEOPLE, INCLUDING TWO CHILDREN.

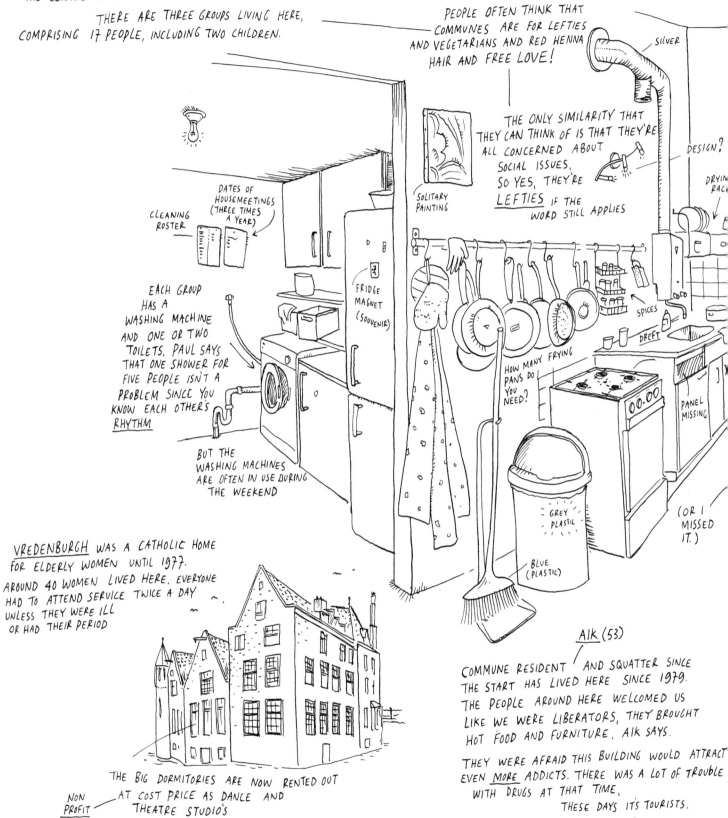

PEOPLE OFTEN THINK THAT COMMUNES ARE FOR LEFTIES AND VEGETARIANS AND RED HENNA HAIR AND FREE LOVE!

SILVER

THE ONLY SIMILARITY THAT THEY CAN THINK OF IS THAT THEY'RE ALL CONCERNED ABOUT SOCIAL ISSUES. SO YES, THEY'RE <u>LEFTIES</u> IF THE WORD STILL APPLIES

DESIGN?

DRYING RACK

SOLITARY PAINTING

DATES OF HOUSEMEETINGS (THREE TIMES A YEAR)

CLEANING ROSTER

FRIDGE MAGNET (SOUVENIR)

SPICES

DREFT

EACH GROUP HAS A WASHING MACHINE AND ONE OR TWO TOILETS. PAUL SAYS THAT ONE SHOWER FOR FIVE PEOPLE ISN'T A PROBLEM SINCE YOU KNOW EACH OTHER'S RHYTHM

HOW MANY FRYING PANS DO YOU NEED?

PANEL MISSING

BUT THE WASHING MACHINES ARE OFTEN IN USE DURING THE WEEKEND

GREY PLASTIC

(OR I MISSED IT.)

BLUE (PLASTIC)

<u>VREDENBURGH</u> WAS A CATHOLIC HOME FOR ELDERLY WOMEN UNTIL 1977. AROUND 40 WOMEN LIVED HERE. EVERYONE HAD TO ATTEND SERVICE TWICE A DAY UNLESS THEY WERE ILL OR HAD THEIR PERIOD

AIK (53)

COMMUNE RESIDENT AND SQUATTER SINCE THE START HAS LIVED HERE SINCE 1979. THE PEOPLE AROUND HERE WELCOMED US LIKE WE WERE LIBERATORS, THEY BROUGHT HOT FOOD AND FURNITURE, AIK SAYS.

THEY WERE AFRAID THIS BUILDING WOULD ATTRACT EVEN <u>MORE</u> ADDICTS. THERE WAS A LOT OF TROUBLE WITH DRUGS AT THAT TIME,

THESE DAYS IT'S TOURISTS.

THE BIG DORMITORIES ARE NOW RENTED OUT AT COST PRICE AS DANCE AND THEATRE STUDIO'S

NON PROFIT

COMMUNE

Around 1980 was the heyday of Holland's squatters, with over 1,000 squats in Amsterdam. In 1985, the city began turning squatters into tenants, leaving many of the buildings standing. In 2010, squatting was made illegal. There are c. 275 squats left in Holland.

ALLOTMENTS

This bit of Southeast Amsterdam is on the edge of the map. For years, no one knew for sure whether it belonged to Amsterdam or North Holland province. Meanwhile, a utopian community emerged here with its own rules and even a mayor.

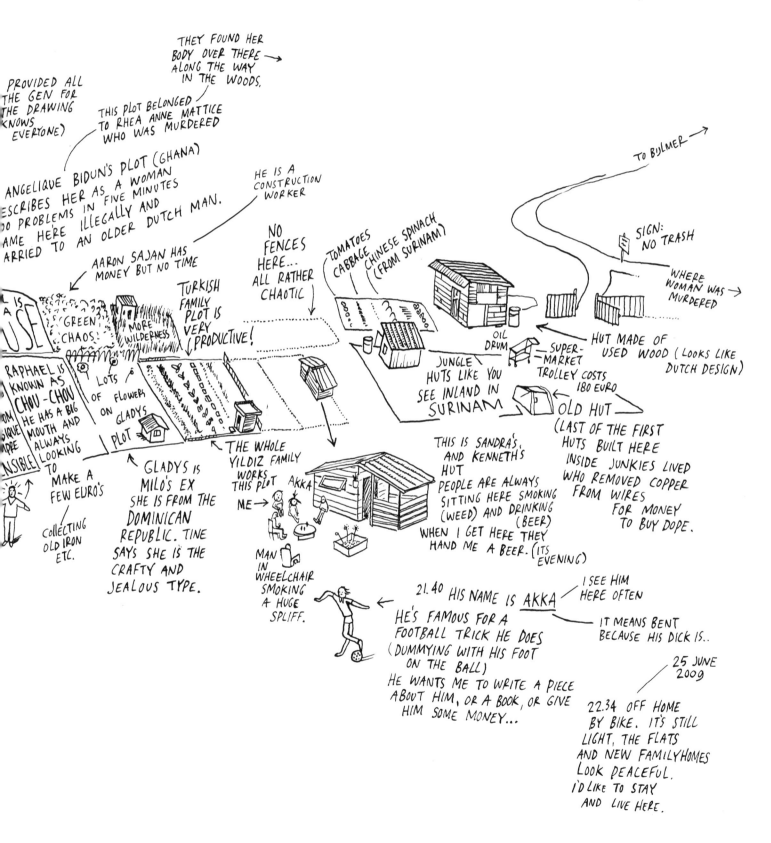

THEY FOUND HER BODY OVER THERE → ALONG THE WAY IN THE WOODS.

PROVIDED ALL THE GEN FOR THE DRAWING (NOWS EVERYONE)

THIS PLOT BELONGED TO RHEA ANNE MATTICE WHO WAS MURDERED

ANGELIQUE BIDUN'S PLOT (GHANA) ESCRIBES HER AS A WOMAN O PROBLEMS IN FIVE MINUTES AME HERE ILLEGALLY AND ARRIED TO AN OLDER DUTCH MAN.

HE IS A CONSTRUCTION WORKER

AARON SAJAN HAS MONEY BUT NO TIME

NO FENCES HERE... ALL RATHER CHAOTIC

TO BULMER →

SIGN: NO TRASH

WHERE WOMAN WAS → MURDERED

TOMATOES CABBAGE CHINESE SPINACH (FROM SURINAM)

TURKISH FAMILY PLOT IS VERY PRODUCTIVE!

A IS USE

GREEN CHAOS

MORE WILDERNESS

LOTS OF FLOWERS ON GLADYS PLOT

RAPHAEL IS KNOWN AS CHOU-CHOU HE HAS A BIG MOUTH AND ALWAYS LOOKING TO MAKE A FEW EURO'S

COLLECTING OLD IRON ETC.

GLADYS IS MILO'S EX SHE IS FROM THE DOMINICAN REPUBLIC. TINE SAYS SHE IS THE CRAFTY AND JEALOUS TYPE.

THE WHOLE YILDIZ FAMILY WORKS THIS PLOT

AKKA

ME →

MAN IN WHEELCHAIR SMOKING A HUGE SPLIFF.

OIL DRUM

SUPER-MARKET TROLLEY COSTS 180 EURO

JUNGLE HUTS LIKE YOU SEE INLAND IN SURINAM

HUT MADE OF USED WOOD (LOOKS LIKE DUTCH DESIGN)

OLD HUT (LAST OF THE FIRST HUTS BUILT HERE INSIDE JUNKIES LIVED WHO REMOVED COPPER FROM WIRES FOR MONEY TO BUY DOPE.

THIS IS SANDRA'S AND KENNETH'S HUT PEOPLE ARE ALWAYS SITTING HERE SMOKING (WEED) AND DRINKING (BEER) WHEN I GET HERE THEY HAND ME A BEER. (ITS EVENING)

21.40 HIS NAME IS AKKA

I SEE HIM HERE OFTEN

HE'S FAMOUS FOR A FOOTBALL TRICK HE DOES (DUMMYING WITH HIS FOOT ON THE BALL) HE WANTS ME TO WRITE A PIECE ABOUT HIM, OR A BOOK, OR GIVE HIM SOME MONEY...

IT MEANS BENT BECAUSE HIS DICK IS..

25 JUNE 2009

22.34 OFF HOME BY BIKE. IT'S STILL LIGHT, THE FLATS AND NEW FAMILYHOMES LOOK PEACEFUL. I'D LIKE TO STAY AND LIVE HERE.

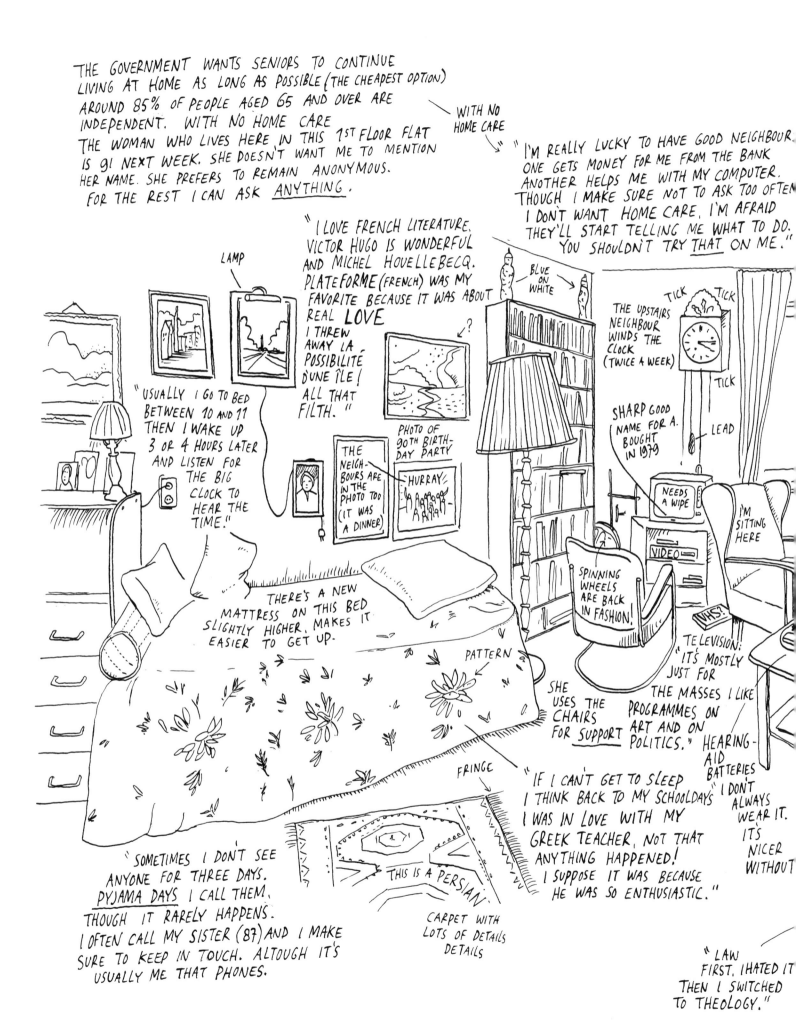

PYJAMA DAYS

Holland is aging. In ten years time, a quarter of the population will be 65 or older. But not in Amsterdam. Here the number of people aged 65 and over is falling, since many who are now reaching that age bracket left the city in the 1970s and 80s.

"AFTER BREAKFAST I OFTEN LIE DOWN FOR A BIT. GATHERING MY STRENGTH TO WASH AND DRESS. I WASH WITH A FLANNEL. ALTHOUGH I'VE GOT A SPECIAL SHOWER CHAIR, I KEEP IT SIMPLE AND DON'T SHOWER VERY OFTEN.
THEN AROUND ELEVEN I'M DRESSED AND HAVE A CUP OF COFFEE."

"AROUND 20.00, I COOK SOMETHING FOR MYSELF. CAULIFLOWER TONIGHT, WITHOUT SAUCE. I'VE KEPT HEALTHY ALL MY LIFE. FOR DESSERT, YOGHURT. THE BOY WHO WORKS AT THE SUPERMARKET DELIVERS MY GROCERIES."

KITCHEN

MALEVICH

NET CURTAIN

HOOKS LOOSE

CHRIST- MAS ROSE

TILES

8:45 BREAKFAST 2 DRY RUSKS AND TWO SAND- WICHES 1 CHEESE 1 JAM

GOLD COLOURED

МАЛЕВИЧ MANET HODIC

STOPPED

WHITE CUSHION

TRAY

PHOTO OF PARENTS?

WINE GLASS

CACTUS (A GIFT)

PHOTO OF BROTHER

TRAVELGUIDE (ROME)

TOASTER

THE 'ENKHUIZER' ALMANAC (ALWAYS THE SAME)

BOX OF OIL PAINTS

PHOTO BOOK OF PICTURES TAKEN AND PRINTED BY A FRIEND

ZIMMER FRAME AND DRYING RACK

LOOSE SCREW

CHAIR WITH LOTS OF BLANKETS AND CUSHIONS

"ONCE YOU REACH 80 PEOPLE START DYING."

"I'M NOT AFRAID. IT WOULD BE A PITY TO DIE. THIS IS A PLEASANT PERIOD. NO OBLIGATIONS. I JUST ENJOY. I HOPE IT HAPPENS HERE AT HOME IN MY SLEEP."

"A COUPLE OF YEARS AGO I BROKE MY HIP. YOUR DYNAMIC BALANCE GOES AS YOU GET OLDER. HAPPENS TO US ALL."

BAG FOR OUTDOORS (WITH ZIP)

AFTER SCHOOL I WENT TO UNIVERSITY... THEN I WENT INTO SOCIAL WORK. I WANTED TO BE A TEACHER. BUT ONLY REALISED THAT LATER. THESE DAYS PEOPLE TAKE A SABBATICAL, OR THEY GO TO NEPAL TO FIND THEMSELVES.

FUNNY (LEGS)

"I THINK REINCARNATION IS MOST PROBABLE. ALTHOUGH I DON'T LIKE THE IDEA. IT REMINDS ME OF A DREAM IN WHICH I'M SOMEWHERE I CAN'T GET OUT OF."

AP
RE

PAINT

There are cat cities and dog cities. In dog cities, you throw a stick and it comes back with its tail wagging. Cat cities are reticent and harder to judge. Amsterdam seems to be a dog city at first, until you discover that it's really a cat city pretending to be a dog.

MASSAGE LI

Massage parlours have become hugely popular in Amsterdam in the last decade. There used to be thirty; now there's three hundred. The police suspect that many Chinese and Oriental massage parlours are actually a front for illegal prostitution and exploitation.

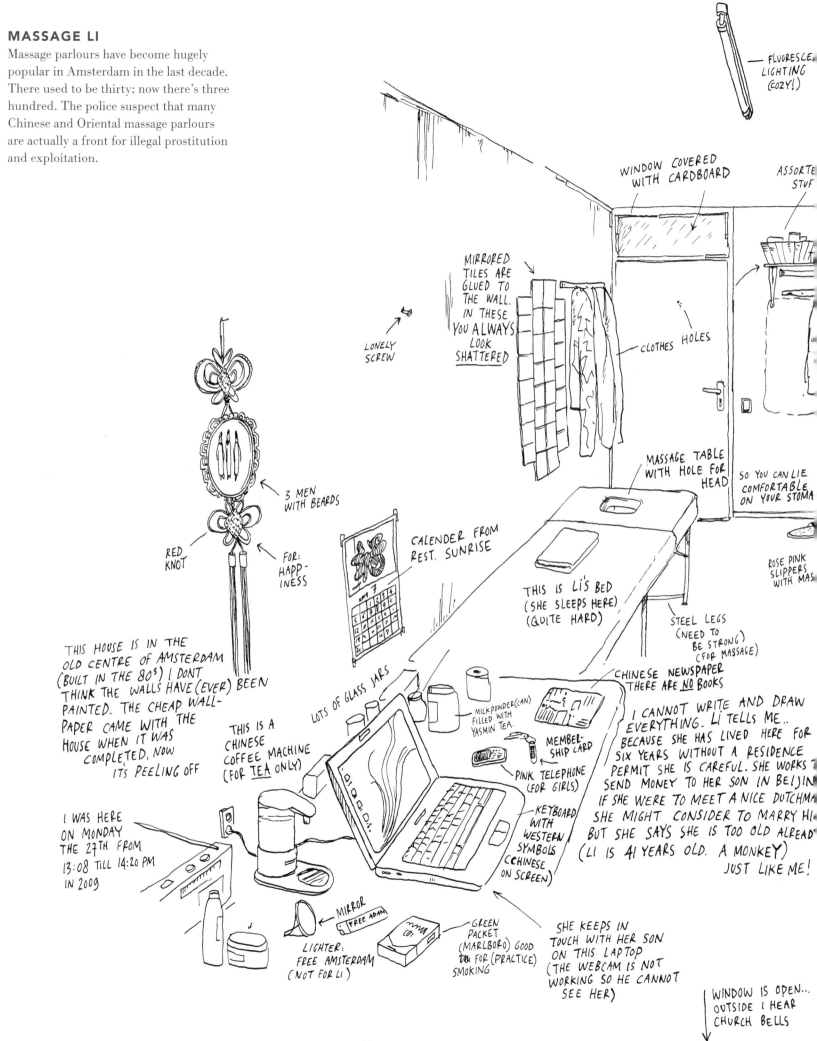

FLUORESCE LIGHTING (COZY!)

WINDOW COVERED WITH CARDBOARD

ASSORTE STUF

MIRRORED TILES ARE GLUED TO THE WALL. IN THESE YOU ALWAYS LOOK SHATTERED

LONELY SCREW

CLOTHES HOLES

MASSAGE TABLE WITH HOLE FOR HEAD

SO YOU CAN LIE COMFORTABLE ON YOUR STOMA

3 MEN WITH BEARDS

RED KNOT

FOR: HAPP- INESS

CALENDER FROM REST. SUNRISE

ROSE PINK SLIPPERS WITH MAS

THIS IS LI'S BED (SHE SLEEPS HERE) (QUITE HARD)

STEEL LEGS (NEED TO BE STRONG) (FOR MASSAGE)

THIS HOUSE IS IN THE OLD CENTRE OF AMSTERDAM (BUILT IN THE 80ˢ) I DONT THINK THE WALLS HAVE (EVER) BEEN PAINTED. THE CHEAP WALL- PAPER CAME WITH THE HOUSE WHEN IT WAS COMPLETED, NOW ITS PEELING OFF

LOTS OF GLASS JARS

THIS IS A CHINESE COFFEE MACHINE (FOR TEA ONLY)

MILK POWDER (CAN) FILLED WITH YASMIN TEA.

MEMBER- SHIP CARD

PINK TELEPHONE (FOR GIRLS)

CHINESE NEWSPAPER THERE ARE NO BOOKS

KEYBOARD WITH WESTERN SYMBOLS (CHINESE ON SCREEN)

I CANNOT WRITE AND DRAW EVERYTHING. LI TELLS ME.. BECAUSE SHE HAS LIVED HERE FOR SIX YEARS WITHOUT A RESIDENCE PERMIT SHE IS CAREFUL. SHE WORKS T SEND MONEY TO HER SON IN BEIJIN IF SHE WERE TO MEET A NICE DUTCHMA SHE MIGHT CONSIDER TO MARRY HI BUT SHE SAYS SHE IS TOO OLD ALREAD (LI IS 41 YEARS OLD. A MONKEY) JUST LIKE ME!

I WAS HERE ON MONDAY THE 27TH FROM 13:08 TILL 14:20 PM IN 2009

MIRROR FREE ADAM

LIGHTER: FREE AMSTERDAM (NOT FOR LI)

GREEN PACKET (MARLBORO) GOOD FOR (PRACTICE) SMOKING

SHE KEEPS IN TOUCH WITH HER SON ON THIS LAPTOP (THE WEBCAM IS NOT WORKING SO HE CANNOT SEE HER)

WINDOW IS OPEN... OUTSIDE I HEAR CHURCH BELLS

THE WALLPAPER IS
LOOSE (THE TAPE TOO)

BROWNISH
CURTAIN

PLASTIC BAGS
SHOEBOXES AND
THINGS LIKE THAT...

WHITE
CLOSET

THIS IS FOR
A STRIP
LAMP

PLASTIC
BEHIND
HAT RACK
WALL OR
CLOTHES
DIRTY?

PICTURE OF BASKETBALL-TEAM:
ALL SMILING (CHINESE) MEN.
BECAUSE OF THE SMILING THEIR
EYES SEEM EVEN SMALLER!
(LINES)

GONIGO

FOLDING CHAIR

BED TO DRY CLOTHES
ON (FOLDED)

BLANKETS

HIS BED BELONGS TO THE WOMAN
SHARES THIS ROOM WITH.
EY SHARE THE RENT OF
0 EURO'S FOR THIS ROOM
THE DAYTIME HER
OMMATE WORKS
ND AT NIGHT
E OFTEN GOES
UT DANCING
AND DRINKING)
HICH MAKES
ER SNORE!

Li USED TO WORK IN A
MASSAGE PARLOR (NO SEX) BUT THE POLICE
RAIDED THE PLACE LOOKING FOR ILLEGAL
IMMIGRANTS. AFTER A FEW MONTHS SHE
WAS BACK. NOW SHE WORKS IN A MASSAGE PARLOUR
OUTSIDE THE CITY, IN A SMALL TOWN. HERE SHE GIVES
WEIGHT-LOSS BELLY MASSAGES
RUBBING WOMENS BELLIES IN ORDER TO
BURN FAT. (DOES THIS WORK?
IS THIS POSSIBLE...)

CAREFULLY
FOLDED
BLANKET

IN THE CORNER
MORE PLASTIC BAGS
WITH CLOTHES?

SNOOPY DUVET COVER SAYS:
ITS GREAT TO BE A CHAMPION

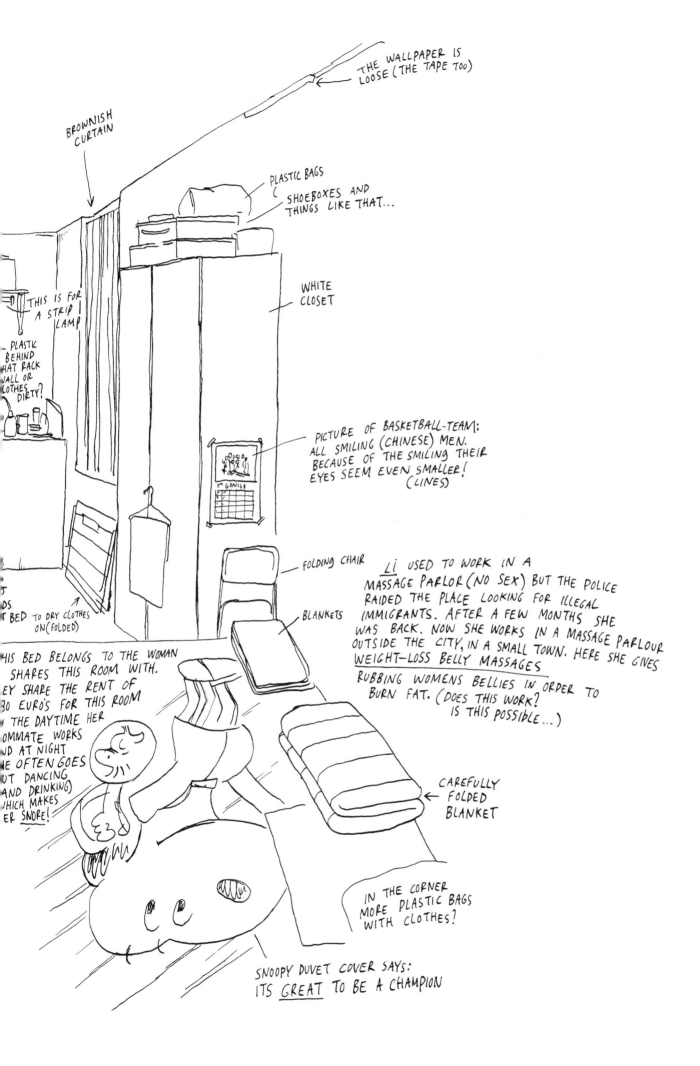

47

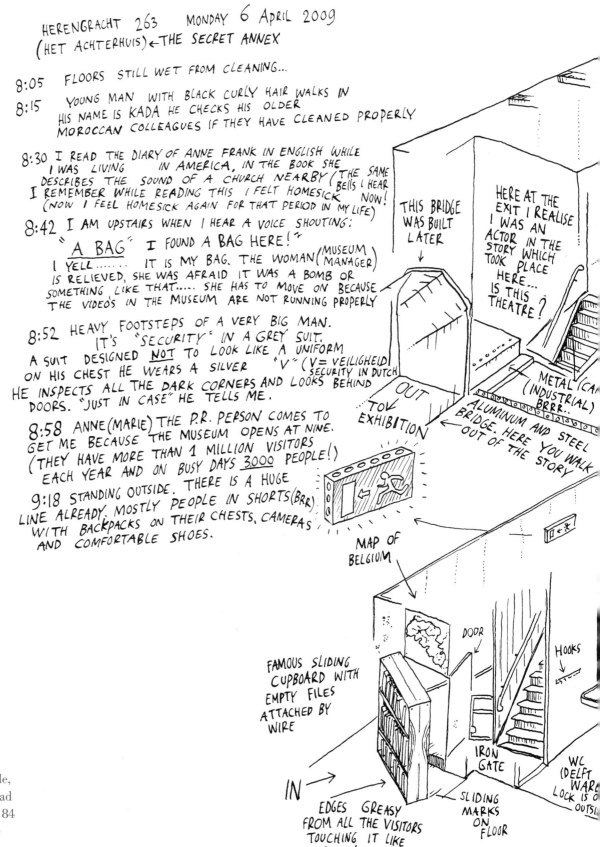

HERENGRACHT 263   MONDAY 6 APRIL 2009
(HET ACHTERHUIS) ← THE SECRET ANNEX

8:05   FLOORS STILL WET FROM CLEANING...

8:15   YOUNG MAN WITH BLACK CURLY HAIR WALKS IN
HIS NAME IS KADA HE CHECKS HIS OLDER
MOROCCAN COLLEAGUES IF THEY HAVE CLEANED PROPERLY

8:30   I READ THE DIARY OF ANNE FRANK IN ENGLISH WHILE
I WAS LIVING   IN AMERICA, IN THE BOOK SHE
DESCRIBES THE SOUND OF A CHURCH NEARBY (THE SAME
I REMEMBER WHILE READING THIS I FELT HOMESICK / BELLS I HEAR
(NOW I FEEL HOMESICK AGAIN FOR THAT PERIOD IN MY LIFE) NOW!

8:42   I AM UPSTAIRS WHEN I HEAR A VOICE SHOUTING:
"A BAG" I FOUND A BAG HERE!
I YELL....... IT IS MY BAG. THE WOMAN (MUSEUM MANAGER)
IS RELIEVED, SHE WAS AFRAID IT WAS A BOMB OR
SOMETHING LIKE THAT..... SHE HAS TO MOVE ON BECAUSE
THE VIDEO'S IN THE MUSEUM ARE NOT RUNNING PROPERLY

8:52   HEAVY FOOTSTEPS OF A VERY BIG MAN.
IT'S "SECURITY" IN A GREY SUIT.
A SUIT DESIGNED NOT TO LOOK LIKE A UNIFORM
ON HIS CHEST HE WEARS A SILVER "V" (V= VEILIGHEID
SECURITY IN DUTCH)
HE INSPECTS ALL THE DARK CORNERS AND LOOKS BEHIND
DOORS. "JUST IN CASE" HE TELLS ME.

8:58   ANNE (MARIE) THE P.R. PERSON COMES TO
GET ME BECAUSE THE MUSEUM OPENS AT NINE.
(THEY HAVE MORE THAN 1 MILLION VISITORS
EACH YEAR AND ON BUSY DAYS 3000 PEOPLE!)

9:18   STANDING OUTSIDE. THERE IS A HUGE
LINE ALREADY. MOSTLY PEOPLE IN SHORTS (BRR)
WITH BACKPACKS ON THEIR CHESTS, CAMERAS
AND COMFORTABLE SHOES.

THIS BRIDGE
WAS BUILT
LATER

HERE AT THE
EXIT I REALISE
I WAS AN
ACTOR IN THE
STORY WHICH
TOOK PLACE
HERE...
IS THIS
THEATRE?

OUT
TO EXHIBITION

METAL (CA
(INDUSTRIAL)
BRRR...
ALUMINUM AND STEEL
BRIDGE. HERE YOU WALK
OUT OF THE STORY

MAP OF
BELGIUM

DOOR

HOOKS

FAMOUS SLIDING
CUPBOARD WITH
EMPTY FILES
ATTACHED BY
WIRE

IRON
GATE

WC
(DELFT
WARE
LOCK IS O
OUTSI

IN →

EDGES GREASY
FROM ALL THE VISITORS
TOUCHING IT LIKE
A RELIC!

SLIDING
MARKS
ON
FLOOR

ANNE FRANK HOUSE

Anne Frank's diary is in the top ten of
the best read books, along with the Bible,
Harry Potter and the Da Vinci Code. Had
she lived, Anne Frank would have been 84
in 2013. In that year, 1.2 million people
visited the secret annex on
the Prinsengracht.

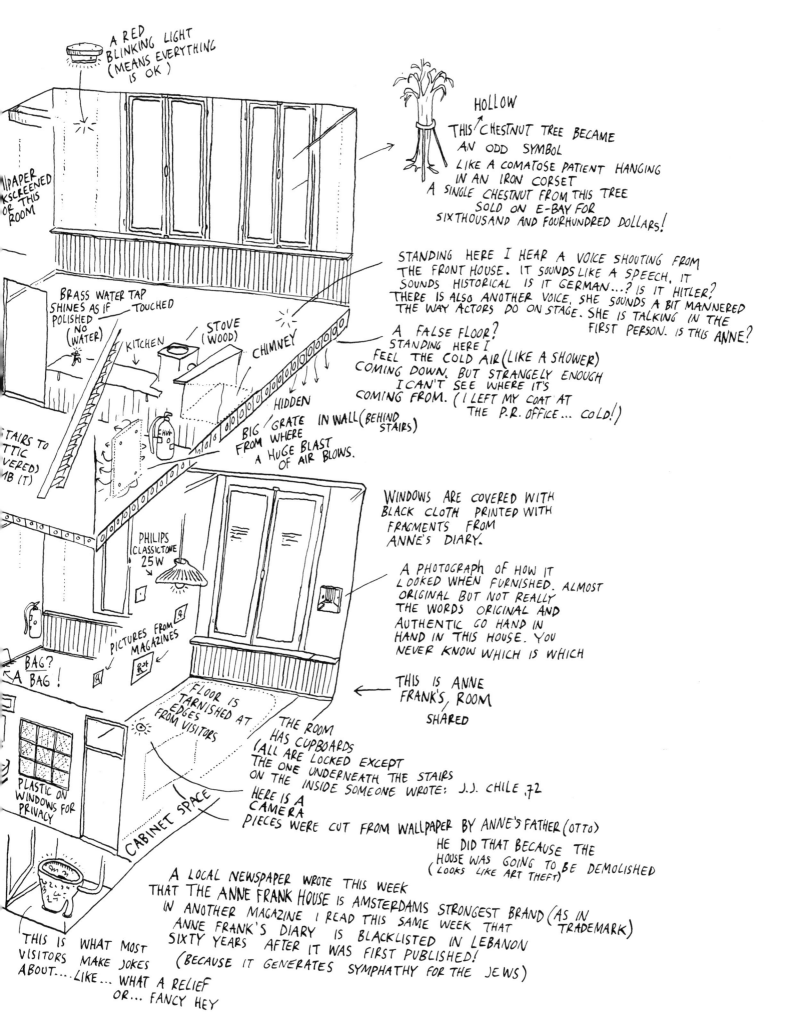

A RED BLINKING LIGHT (MEANS EVERYTHING IS OK)

HOLLOW

THIS CHESTNUT TREE BECAME AN ODD SYMBOL LIKE A COMATOSE PATIENT HANGING IN AN IRON CORSET A SINGLE CHESTNUT FROM THIS TREE SOLD ON E-BAY FOR SIXTHOUSAND AND FOURHUNDRED DOLLARS!

...PAPER ...KSCREENED ...OR THIS ROOM

BRASS WATER TAP SHINES AS IF TOUCHED POLISHED NO (WATER)

KITCHEN

STOVE (WOOD)

CHIMNEY

HIDDEN

STANDING HERE I HEAR A VOICE SHOUTING FROM THE FRONT HOUSE. IT SOUNDS LIKE A SPEECH, IT SOUNDS HISTORICAL IS IT GERMAN...? IS IT HITLER? THERE IS ALSO ANOTHER VOICE, SHE SOUNDS A BIT MANNERED THE WAY ACTORS DO ON STAGE. SHE IS TALKING IN THE FIRST PERSON. IS THIS ANNE?

A FALSE FLOOR? STANDING HERE I FEEL THE COLD AIR (LIKE A SHOWER) COMING DOWN. BUT STRANGELY ENOUGH I CAN'T SEE WHERE IT'S COMING FROM. (I LEFT MY COAT AT THE P.R. OFFICE... COLD!)

BIG GRATE IN WALL (BEHIND STAIRS) FROM WHERE A HUGE BLAST OF AIR BLOWS.

...TAIRS TO ...TTIC ...VERED) ...MB (T)

PHILIPS CLASSICTONE 25W

WINDOWS ARE COVERED WITH BLACK CLOTH PRINTED WITH FRAGMENTS FROM ANNE'S DIARY.

A PHOTOGRAPH OF HOW IT LOOKED WHEN FURNISHED. ALMOST ORIGINAL BUT NOT REALLY THE WORDS ORIGINAL AND AUTHENTIC GO HAND IN HAND IN THIS HOUSE. YOU NEVER KNOW WHICH IS WHICH

PICTURES FROM MAGAZINES

BAG? A BAG!

THIS IS ANNE FRANK'S ROOM SHARED

FLOOR IS TARNISHED AT EDGES FROM VISITORS

PLASTIC ON WINDOWS FOR PRIVACY

CABINET SPACE

THE ROOM HAS CUPBOARDS (ALL ARE LOCKED EXCEPT THE ONE UNDERNEATH THE STAIRS ON THE INSIDE SOMEONE WROTE: J.J. CHILE .72

HERE IS A CAMERA

PIECES WERE CUT FROM WALLPAPER BY ANNE'S FATHER (OTTO) HE DID THAT BECAUSE THE HOUSE WAS GOING TO BE DEMOLISHED (LOOKS LIKE ART THEFT)

A LOCAL NEWSPAPER WROTE THIS WEEK THAT THE ANNE FRANK HOUSE IS AMSTERDAMS STRONGEST BRAND (AS IN TRADEMARK) IN ANOTHER MAGAZINE I READ THIS SAME WEEK THAT ANNE FRANK'S DIARY IS BLACKLISTED IN LEBANON SIXTY YEARS AFTER IT WAS FIRST PUBLISHED!

THIS IS WHAT MOST VISITORS MAKE JOKES ABOUT.... LIKE... WHAT A RELIEF OR... FANCY HEY

(BECAUSE IT GENERATES SYMPHATHY FOR THE JEWS)

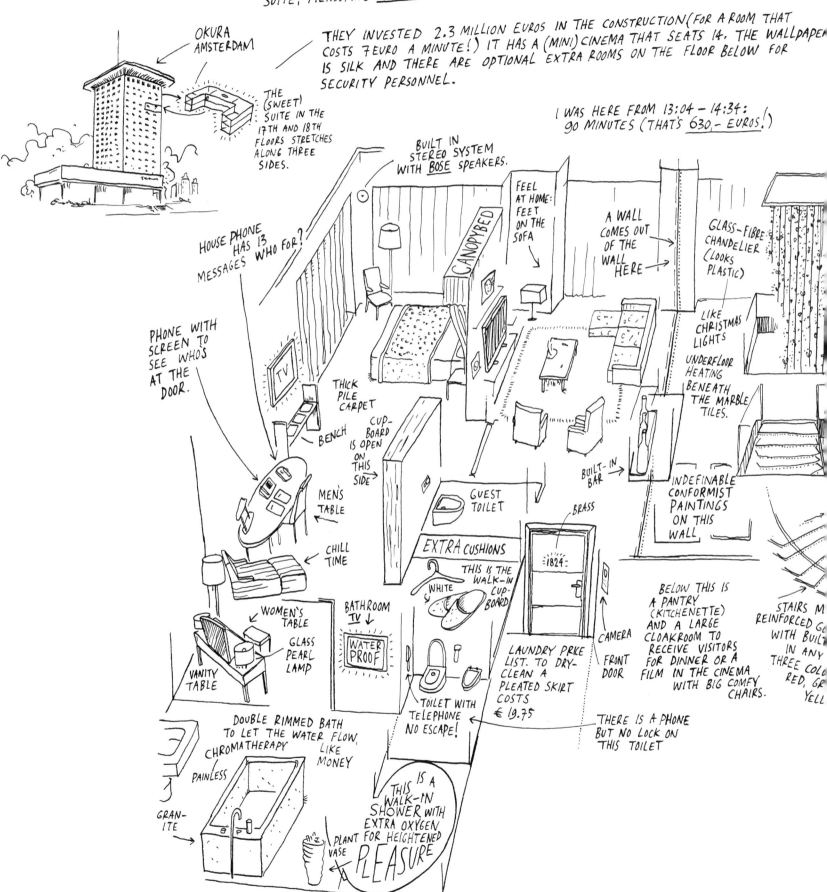

OKURA SCRAPPED 18 HOTEL ROOMS TO CREATE BENELUX'S MOST LUXURIOUS SUITE, MEASURING 485 M² (TENNIS COURTS ARE 260 M²).

THEY INVESTED 2.3 MILLION EUROS IN THE CONSTRUCTION (FOR A ROOM THAT COSTS 7EURO A MINUTE!) IT HAS A (MINI) CINEMA THAT SEATS 14. THE WALLPAPER IS SILK AND THERE ARE OPTIONAL EXTRA ROOMS ON THE FLOOR BELOW FOR SECURITY PERSONNEL.

OKURA AMSTERDAM

THE (SWEET) SUITE IN THE 17TH AND 18TH FLOORS STRETCHES ALONG THREE SIDES.

I WAS HERE FROM 13:04 - 14:34: 90 MINUTES (THAT'S 630,- EUROS!)

BUILT IN STEREO SYSTEM WITH BOSE SPEAKERS.

HOUSE PHONE HAS 13 MESSAGES WHO FOR?

PHONE WITH SCREEN TO SEE WHO'S AT THE DOOR.

CANOPYBED

FEEL AT HOME: FEET ON THE SOFA

A WALL COMES OUT OF THE WALL HERE

GLASS-FIBRE CHANDELIER (LOOKS PLASTIC)

LIKE CHRISTMAS LIGHTS

UNDERFLOOR HEATING BENEATH THE MARBLE TILES.

TV

THICK PILE CARPET

CUP-BOARD IS OPEN ON THIS SIDE

BENCH

MEN'S TABLE

CHILL TIME

GUEST TOILET

BUILT-IN BAR

INDEFINABLE CONFORMIST PAINTINGS ON THIS WALL

EXTRA CUSHIONS

THIS IS THE WALK-IN CUP-BOARD

WHITE

1824

BRASS

BELOW THIS IS A PANTRY (KITCHENETTE) AND A LARGE CLOAKROOM TO RECEIVE VISITORS FOR DINNER OR A FILM IN THE CINEMA WITH BIG COMFY CHAIRS.

STAIRS M REINFORCED G WITH BUIL IN ANY THREE COL RED, GR YELL

WOMEN'S TABLE

GLASS PEARL LAMP

VANITY TABLE

BATHROOM TV ↓

WATER PROOF

CAMERA

FRONT DOOR

LAUNDRY PRICE LIST. TO DRY-CLEAN A PLEATED SKIRT COSTS € 19.75

THERE IS A PHONE BUT NO LOCK ON THIS TOILET

TOILET WITH TELEPHONE NO ESCAPE!

DOUBLE RIMMED BATH TO LET THE WATER FLOW, LIKE MONEY

CHROMATHERAPY

PAINLESS

GRAN-ITE

THIS IS A WALK-IN SHOWER WITH EXTRA OXYGEN PLANT FOR HEIGHTENED PLEASURE

VASE

There are 413 hotels in Amsterdam, with around 55,000 beds. Average price for a night in a hotel is 132 euros. Meanwhile, more people are renting out rooms or even their whole house via websites such as Airbnb and Wimdu.

"THE SUITE" MAKES SURE YOU DON'T OVERSPEND: IT DIVIDES INTO SMALLER UNITS. SOUNDPROOF WALLS DRAWN ALONG THE DOTTED LINE SEAL OFF A SECTION

THE BEDSIDE TABLE DRAWER HAS A BIBLE AND THE TEACHINGS OF BUDDHA. NO QURAN THOUGH...

RED CORAL

RATHER NICE

BIBLE

BUDDHA

NICE VIEW OF AMSTER-DAM

(DARK) SILK SHINY WALL-PAPER

THE SUITE COSTS 416 EUROS AN HOUR (10,000 EUROS A NIGHT) A CONTINENTAL BREAKFAST COSTS 29,50 EUROS (EXTRA), THOUGH IF YOUR SPENDING THAT KIND OF MONEY...

BURN MARK IN CARPET

BAR

AIRS DINING-OM AND EMA, HICH SEATS 4

SOMEONE SECRETLY SMOKED AT THE OPEN WINDOW

NO MINI-BOTTLES IN THE BAR— THESE ARE ADULT SIZE

THEY'RE HIGHLY DISCREET ABOUT THE CELEBRITIES THAT HAVE USED THE SUITE, BUT I'VE HEARD THAT THE DALAI LAMA SLEPT HERE RECENTLY...

HI-TECH TOUCH SCREEN TO OPERATE THE CURTAINS, TV, SPEAKERS AND AIRCONDITIONING

LEATHER

GREASY FINGER PRINT BELONGS TO... GUEST TOILET

BOOKS— NOT FOR READING BUT TO LEAF THROUGH

PUFF

SUNLIGHT ENTERS AT 14.10

THERE

THE BIG TABLE IS UNDER THE CHANDELIER

DO NOT DISTURB

THIS WALK-IN WARDROBE IS THE SIZE OF AN AVERAGE BEDROOM IN THE HOUSES AROUND HERE THE WARDROBE IS SO BIG MY CLOTHES WOULD FEEL NAKED IN IT.

PUFF

PUFF

VLADIMIR PUTIN, SANDRA BULLOCK AND THE DALAI LAMA SWEATED HERE...

NO NEED TO SHUT THE BATHROOM CURTAINS... NO NEIGHBOURS (FAR TOO HIGH)

MPS

DECORATION (OLD COCONUTS)

HERE OKURA SERVES MICHELIN STAR MEALS FROM "LE CIEL BLEU" RESTAURANT ON THE 23RD FLOOR (COSTS EXTRA OF COURSE)

IF I LEFT THEM THERE ALONE (MY CLOTHES)

SHELL-SHAPED WALK-IN SHOWER WITH TINY SHINY STONES

BATHTUB IS EGG SHAPED (FOR REBIRTHING)

THE MIRRORS ARE HEATED TO PREVENT CONDEN-SATION.

MIRROR IMAGE

DRAIN

VERY NICE!

BATHROOM PRODUCTS ARE BY L'OCCITANE

BACK OF TV

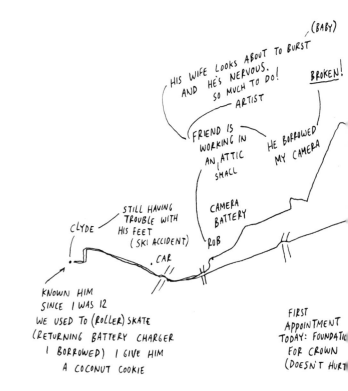

BIG DAY, LITTLE CHORES

The advantage of a small city is that everything is a short bike-ride away. But it's
not always obvious which way is quickest.
The circular canals dictate the street plan
far into the suburbs, so it can be hard to
cycle like the crow flies in a twisting city.

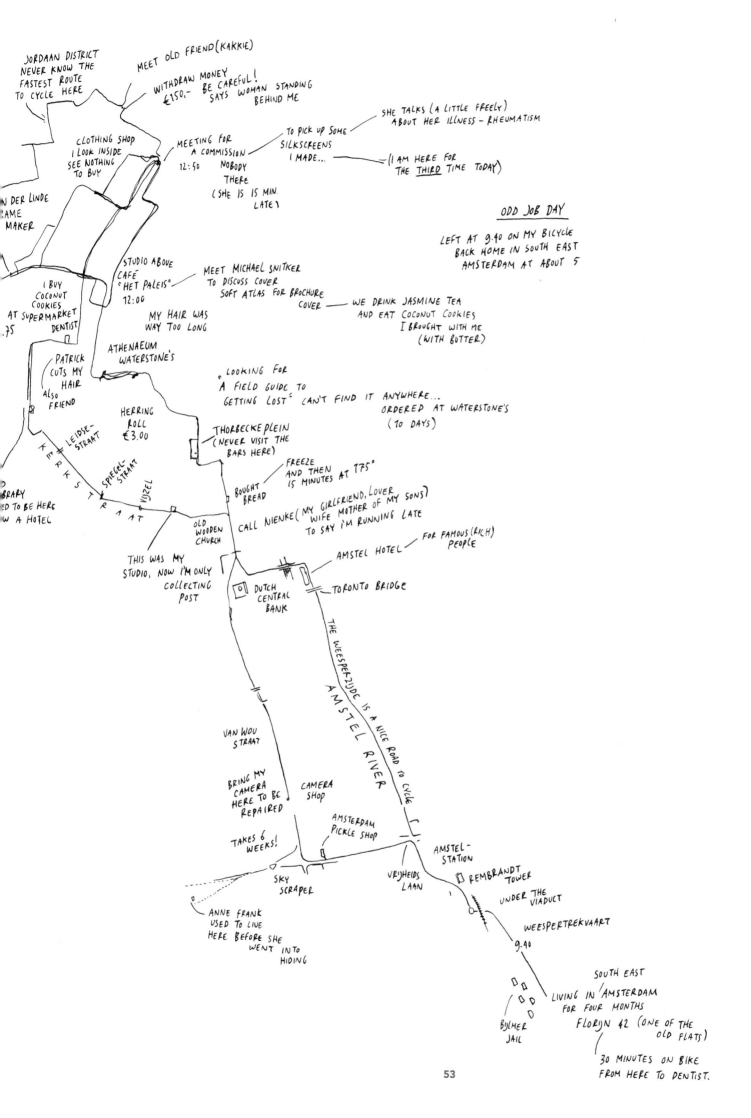

JORDAAN DISTRICT
NEVER KNOW THE
FASTEST ROUTE
TO CYCLE HERE

MEET OLD FRIEND (KAKKIE)

WITHDRAW MONEY
€150,- BE CAREFUL!
SAYS WOMAN STANDING
BEHIND ME

CLOTHING SHOP
I LOOK INSIDE
SEE NOTHING
TO BUY

MEETING FOR
A COMMISSION
12:50   NOBODY
          THERE
      (SHE IS 15 MIN.
          LATE)

TO PICK UP SOME
SILKSCREENS
I MADE...

SHE TALKS (A LITTLE FREELY)
ABOUT HER ILLNESS - RHEUMATISM

(I AM HERE FOR
THE THIRD TIME TODAY)

N DER LINDE
AME
MAKER

I BUY
COCONUT
COOKIES
AT SUPERMARKET
.75   DENTIST

STUDIO ABOVE
CAFÉ
"HET PALEIS"
12:00

MEET MICHAEL SNITKER
TO DISCUSS COVER
SOFT ATLAS FOR BROCHURE
COVER

MY HAIR WAS
WAY TOO LONG

ODD JOB DAY

LEFT AT 9.40 ON MY BICYCLE
BACK HOME IN SOUTH EAST
AMSTERDAM AT ABOUT 5

WE DRINK JASMINE TEA
AND EAT COCONUT COOKIES
I BROUGHT WITH ME
(WITH BUTTER)

PATRICK
CUTS MY
HAIR
ALSO
FRIEND

ATHENAEUM
WATERSTONE'S

"LOOKING FOR
A FIELD GUIDE TO
GETTING LOST" CAN'T FIND IT ANYWHERE...
            ORDERED AT WATERSTONE'S
                (10 DAYS)

HERRING
ROLL
€3.00

THORBECKE PLEIN
(NEVER VISIT THE
BARS HERE)

K
E   LEIDSE-
R   STRAAT
K
S   SPIEGEL-
T   STRAAT
R   V
A   IJ
A   Z
T   E
           L

BRARY
ED TO BE HERE
W A HOTEL

BOUGHT
BREAD

FREEZE
AND THEN
15 MINUTES AT 175°

OLD
WOODEN
CHURCH

CALL NIENKE (MY GIRLFRIEND, LOVER
            WIFE MOTHER OF MY SONS)
TO SAY I'M RUNNING LATE

AMSTEL HOTEL

FOR FAMOUS (RICH)
PEOPLE

THIS WAS MY
STUDIO, NOW I'M ONLY
COLLECTING
POST

DUTCH
CENTRAL
BANK

TORONTO BRIDGE

T
H
E   W
    E
    E
    S   IS A NICE ROAD TO CYCLE
    P
    E
A   R
M   Z
S   IJ
T   D
E   E
L

R
I
V
E
R

VAN WOU
STRAAT

BRING MY
CAMERA
HERE TO BE
REPAIRED

CAMERA
SHOP

TAKES 6
WEEKS!

AMSTERDAM
PICKLE SHOP

AMSTEL-
STATION

VRIJHEIDS
LAAN

REMBRANDT
TOWER

SKY
SCRAPER

ANNE FRANK
USED TO LIVE
HERE BEFORE SHE
WENT INTO
HIDING

UNDER THE
VIADUCT

WEESPERTREKVAART

9.40

SOUTH EAST

LIVING IN AMSTERDAM
FOR FOUR MONTHS
FLORIJN 42 (ONE OF THE
          OLD FLATS)

BIJLMER
JAIL

30 MINUTES ON BIKE
FROM HERE TO DENTIST.

HOUSEBOAT

People have lived on boats in Amsterdam since the 17th century. In the 1950's there was a great housing shortage, and houseboats became an integral part of the cityscape in that period. Today there are 2500 houseboats in the 156 canals in Amsterdam.

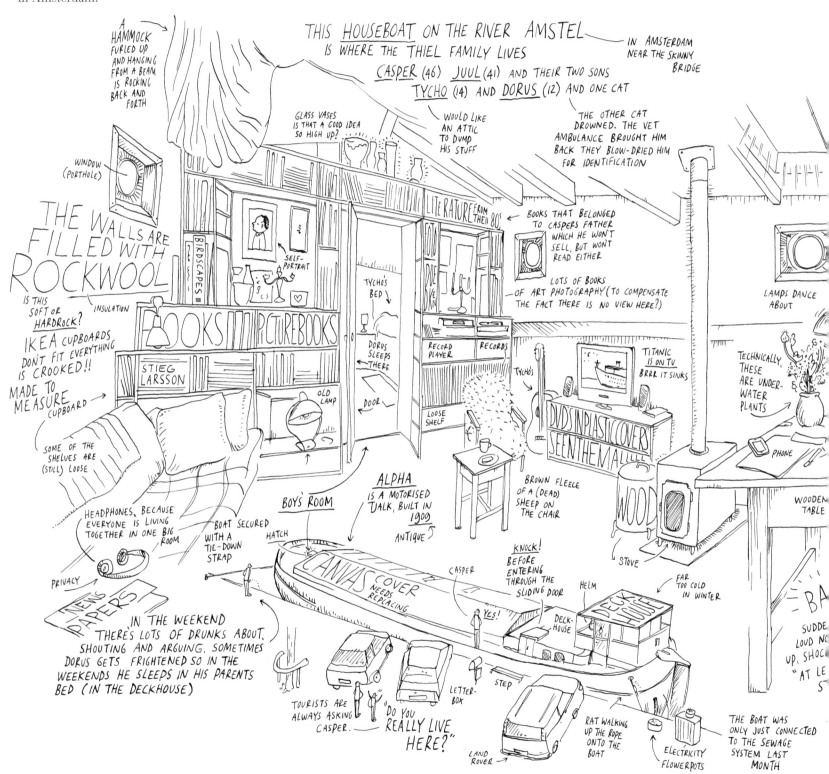

A HAMMOCK FURLED UP AND HANGING FROM A BEAM IS ROCKING BACK AND FORTH

THIS HOUSEBOAT ON THE RIVER AMSTEL IS WHERE THE THIEL FAMILY LIVES

IN AMSTERDAM NEAR THE SKINNY BRIDGE

CASPER (46) JUUL (41) AND THEIR TWO SONS TYCHO (14) AND DORUS (12) AND ONE CAT

GLASS VASES IS THAT A GOOD IDEA SO HIGH UP?

WOULD LIKE AN ATTIC TO DUMP HIS STUFF

THE OTHER CAT DROWNED. THE VET AMBULANCE BROUGHT HIM BACK THEY BLOW-DRIED HIM FOR IDENTIFICATION

WINDOW (PORTHOLE)

LITERATURE FROM THE 80s

BOOKS THAT BELONGED TO CASPERS FATHER WHICH HE WON'T SELL, BUT WON'T READ EITHER

SELF-PORTRAIT

BIRDSCAPES III

THE WALLS ARE FILLED WITH ROCKWOOL

IS THIS SOFT OR HARDROCK?   INSULATION

LOTS OF BOOKS OF ART PHOTOGRAPHY (TO COMPENSATE THE FACT THERE IS NO VIEW HERE?)

LAMPS DANCE ABOUT

IKEA CUPBOARDS DON'T FIT EVERYTHING IS CROOKED!!

MADE TO MEASURE CUPBOARD

BOOKS   PICTUREBOOKS

STIEG LARSSON

TYCHO'S BED

DORUS SLEEPS THERE

RECORD PLAYER   RECORDS

TITANIC IS ON TV BRRR IT SINKS

TECHNICALLY, THESE ARE UNDER-WATER PLANTS

TYCHO'S

SOME OF THE SHELVES ARE (STILL) LOOSE

OLD LAMP

DOOR

LOOSE SHELF

DVDS IN PLASTIC COVER SEEN THEM ALL!!!!

WOOD

PHONE

WOODEN TABLE

HEADPHONES, BECAUSE EVERYONE IS LIVING TOGETHER IN ONE BIG ROOM

BOY'S ROOM

BOAT SECURED WITH A TIE-DOWN STRAP

ALPHA IS A MOTORISED TJALK, BUILT IN 1909 ANTIQUE

BROWN FLEECE OF A (DEAD) SHEEP ON THE CHAIR

STOVE

PRIVACY

HATCH

KNOCK! BEFORE ENTERING THROUGH THE SLIDING DOOR

CASPER

FAR TOO COLD IN WINTER

BA

NEWS PAPERS

CANVAS COVER NEEDS REPLACING

YES!

HELM

DECK HOUSE

SUDDE LOUD NO UP, SHOC "AT LE 5

IN THE WEEKEND THERE'S LOTS OF DRUNKS ABOUT, SHOUTING AND ARGUING, SOMETIMES DORUS GETS FRIGHTENED SO IN THE WEEKENDS HE SLEEPS IN HIS PARENTS BED (IN THE DECKHOUSE)

DECK-HOUSE

TOURISTS ARE ALWAYS ASKING CASPER.

LETTER-BOX

STEP

"DO YOU REALLY LIVE HERE?"

RAT WALKING UP THE ROPE ONTO THE BOAT

ELECTRICITY FLOWERPOTS

THE BOAT WAS ONLY JUST CONNECTED TO THE SEWAGE SYSTEM LAST MONTH

LAND ROVER

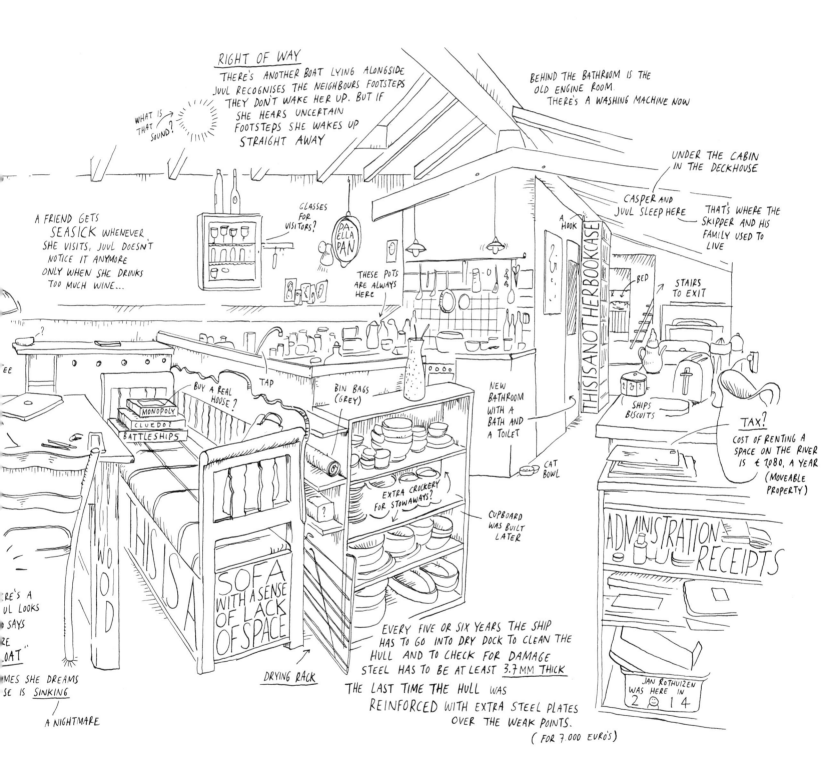

RIGHT OF WAY

THERE'S ANOTHER BOAT LYING ALONGSIDE
JUUL RECOGNISES THE NEIGHBOURS FOOTSTEPS
THEY DON'T WAKE HER UP. BUT IF
SHE HEARS UNCERTAIN
FOOTSTEPS SHE WAKES UP
STRAIGHT AWAY

WHAT IS THAT SOUND?

BEHIND THE BATHROOM IS THE
OLD ENGINE ROOM.
THERE'S A WASHING MACHINE NOW

UNDER THE CABIN
IN THE DECKHOUSE

CASPER AND
JUUL SLEEP HERE

THAT'S WHERE THE
SKIPPER AND HIS
FAMILY USED TO
LIVE

A FRIEND GETS
SEASICK WHENEVER
SHE VISITS, JUUL DOESN'T
NOTICE IT ANYMORE
ONLY WHEN SHE DRINKS
TOO MUCH WINE...

GLASSES
FOR
VISITORS?

PA-
ELLA
PAN

THESE POTS
ARE ALWAYS
HERE

A HOOK

THISISANOTHERBOOKCASE

BED

STAIRS
TO EXIT

BUY A REAL
HOUSE?

MONOPOLY
CLUEDO?
BATTLESHIPS

TAP

BIN BAGS
(GREY)

NEW
BATHROOM
WITH A
BATH AND
A TOILET

CAT
BOWL

SHIPS
BISCUITS

TAX?

COST OF RENTING A
SPACE ON THE RIVER
IS € 1.080, A YEAR
(MOVEABLE
PROPERTY)

THIS IS A SOFA WITH A SENSE OF LACK OF SPACE

W O O D

EXTRA CROCKERY
FOR STOWAWAYS?

CUPBOARD
WAS BUILT
LATER

ADMINISTRATION
RECEIPTS

RE'S A
UL LOOKS
O SAYS
RE
OAT"

MES SHE DREAMS
SE IS SINKING

A NIGHTMARE

DRYING RACK

EVERY FIVE OR SIX YEARS THE SHIP
HAS TO GO INTO DRY DOCK TO CLEAN THE
HULL AND TO CHECK FOR DAMAGE
STEEL HAS TO BE AT LEAST 3.7 MM THICK
THE LAST TIME THE HULL WAS
REINFORCED WITH EXTRA STEEL PLATES
OVER THE WEAK POINTS.
(FOR 7.000 EURO'S)

JAN ROTHUIZEN
WAS HERE IN
2 0 14

MARCH ~~TUES~~ 13 2010
10 PM
SATURDAY NIGHT
IT'S COLD...
4.7° PEOPLE ARE WEARING HATS

ON WINDOW (THIS IS THE BACK OF THE STOCK EXCHANGE)

PEDESTRIANS (UNDER THE INFLUENCE)

NYSE EURONEXT

START
STARTED HERE

BUSY LIKE A COMMERCIAL STREET

HOTEL WINSTON

IS ALSO A NIGHTCLUB
TONIGHT'S MUSIC: PSYCHEDELIC ROCK FROM THE U.S.A

WOMAN DANCES (NAKED) ON TRANSPARANT PLATFORM-SHOES. ON THE BAR. WOW!

TA WARM
MEN O
LA E E N PR

THE GOLDEN (FLEECE) VLIES CONDOMERIE
PEOPLE (TOURISTS) ARE ALWAYS SNIGGERING IN FRONT OF WINDOW

AT THE ENTRANCE IS A PAINTING OF

"RED"
INTERIOR GIFT SHOP WHERE EVERYTHING IS... (REDHEADS GET 10% DISCOUNT)

TRENDY BAKERY
AND COFFEE TO GO (FOR THE PROSTITUTES)

NEON SIGN SMARTSHOP

BUNKBEDS IN CABIN LIKE ROOMS

THIS IS THE NEW GOLDBERGER ALLEY HAS BLACK TILES (OF RUBBER) AGAINST NOISE

HOOKERS.NL
IS A FORUM WHERE PEOPLE WRITE REVIEWS ABOUT... LIKE

ADMISSON € 5.-

BAR

W139
BEHIND THIS FACADE IS A BIG EXHIBITION SPACE FOR YOUNG ART BY ELDERLY ARTISTS.

THEY'RE ALSO HUMAN

THIS TYPE OF SHOP IS SOOO BRIDGE AND TUNNEL LIKE. (PROVINCIAL)

ST. ANNE STR.

RECYCLED

CLOSES AT 22:00

SMART ZONE MUSH ROOMS

HOW SMART (SHOP) CAN YOU GET.

GATE
JENNIFER FROM BULGARIA ONE OF THE PRETTIEST PUSSY'S, NOT SO SPONTANEOUS.

NO PICTURES

STICKER ON WINDOW
CAMERAS

POR INDO

OLD SIGN ON DOOR
ZWART
FABRIC WORKSHOP LOOKS AUTHENTIC "REAL"

THESE BUILDINGS ARE DESOLATE (DISHEVELED) WAITING FOR A FUTURE!

CCTV CAMERA

PEOPLE STANDING

PSSSST

SPANISH SPEAKING (HOOKER) SHOUTS AT CUSTOMERS

BIG BREASTED PLATINUM BLONDE IS ON PHONE WHILE LOOKING AT CLIENTS OUTSIDE

PSSST

ROOF TO PROTECT OPEN DOOR FRO

10:04 PM
GIGGLING DRUNKEN GIRL CROUCHES IN THE STREET TO PEE.

VICKY ROMANIAN BECKY

DIFFERENT SALE STRATEGIES

THERE

WHILE PEOPLE PASS BY

PAMELA FROM GOUDA (CHEESE) 25 YEARS OF FUCKING WAS OBLIGATORY ~~SEX~~ WRITES H. ON HOOKERS.NL (THE WEBSITE)

CHANTALL

SHANIA

THERE IS A HOU SHORTAGE HERE...
SIGNS:
ROOM FOR REN 020-627440S
J. JOINKI
NAME

HOLLOW TOOTH

SCREEN OF THE LUCKY FUTURE

FACADE IS SUPPORTED WITH WOODEN BEAMS

CAMERAS

GATE (CLOSED) OF ALLEY

POSTERS

R SHUTT (HORSE PAIN

RED LIGHT DISTRICT

Most of Amsterdam's estimated 6,000 prostitutes advertise their wares in a window. Around 800 work in sex clubs or privately from home; between 1,200 and 1,400 sex workers find their clients through escort agencies.

WARMOESEST
MEANS A VEGETABLE GARDEN
WOMEN ONLY

11:08 PM
TWO MEN ARE BEING FRISKED
BY THE POLICE, REAL QUICK
(THEY FIND NOTHING...)

COCKRING
WHATEVER YOU WANT
WHEN YOU WANT IT.
(MEN ONLY)

CENTRAL STATION →

OLDER MEN IN BLACK LEATHER
(WHY SO FEW YOUNG MEN IN LEATHER?)

DIRTY NELL SPORTS BAR

HERE PEOPLE FEEL
AT HOME AWAY
FROM HOME

DOWN THE
STREET SEX IS
CELEBRATED (LIBERATED)
CELEBRATED (AT THE COCKRING)

NEW HOUSES
LOOK OLD
ALREADY

TATTOO SHOP

UGA FISH NDA NET GLORIA GHA GUNA

← OUT OF AFRICA

DAY-CARE →
(NOT 24 HRS)

BLACK LADIES SIN:

DURING THE DAY
YOU CAN HAVE YOUR
PICTURE TAKEN
(DRESSED UP AS...)
IN THE WINDOW
(COSTS SOME
MONEY
OFF COURSE)

GLORIA (FROM JAMAICA)
IS WEARING A RED
FISHNET. THERE ARE
NO BRA'S FOR HER SIZE...
SHE WORKS TILL 7AM
(EVERYDAY)

EMERGENCY EXIT

KASBAH
SEX ROOMS
...LOTS
MUSIC...
DILDO
COLORED
CONDOMS

COFFEE MACHINE

PRIVATE CABINS..

EROTIC
SUPER
MARKET

SEXY LAND

BECAUSE OF
INTERNET THE
VIDEO CABINS
ARE CLOSED.

FOLLOW THE
SUNFLOWER

GROUPLEADER
(INDIAN)
← GROUP

MONUMENT
FOR THE
UNKNOWN
PROSTITUTE
(NOT IRONIC)

DING
DONG
DING
DONG

THIS IS THE
OLDEST (STANDING)
BUILDING IN
AMSTERDAM.
IT IS CALLED
A THE 'OLD'
CHURCH

NIEUWE DIJK
NINE DWARS STRAAT

PREMIER LEAGUE

MAN PUKES
(SICK)
PUKE
23:40 PM

FELL OVER
OLD
COBBLE STONES

OLD COBBLE STONES

RED
HANGING
LAMPS
ARE
COZY

PLATINUM BLONDES
SUN BED TAN
STONE FACES

LUNCH ROOM 52

COFFEESHOP

← THE OLD CHURCH

PAMELA HAS HER BOYFRIENDS NAME TATTOOED ABOVE HER BUTTOCKS

PIMP?

ENTRANCE

INSIDE
REMBRANDTS ←
WIFE IS BURIED..
WHERE IS
BURIED?

OUDE KERK

↑ DUTCH NAME

JUST BEGUN
EGG
NITA HAS A
SIGN ON HER
WINDOW!
TO MAKE IT
EASY!

NARROW

TIK TIK

A MAN
SHOUTS

IT'S BUSY AS
RUSH HOUR!
(TRAFFIC JAM)

ELDERLY
YOUNGSTERS (FROM AMERICA!)
TALK ABOUT
JIM MORISSON
"HE IS REALLY MENTAL"

← UNCOMMON
AMSTERDAM
HOUSES

BEWARE!
THESE
CAN DISSAPEAR
INTO THE STREET!

COME HERE!

22:17 PM
I DRINK
TEA (BLACK)

COUNTER FOR
HASH WEED
AND
TRANQUILITEA!

IS THIS A STREET (PUBLIC?)
OR A HALLWAY...
VERY NARROW AND
COVERED

PEDESTRIANS
(AND CHILDREN)
ONLY

TOURISTS COME IN
JUST TO HAVE A LOOK.
SIGN BULLDOG

SOUVENIRS
OF COFFEE-
SHOP

KODAK MOMENT

CLICK CLACK

WHISTLE

FORCED SMILE

CLICK

THE BULLDOG
THE FIRST COFFEESHOP

MOROCCAN
(DOORMAN) SAYS
THE BRITS CANT
HOLD THEIR BEER
THEY COME HERE
ON STAG NIGHTS

22:10 PM
MAN RUMMAGES
THROUGH TRASH.
YOU NEVER KNOW!

22:40 PM
INFALATABLE
PENIS THEY (BRITISH)
GIRLS THINK ITS
HILARIOUS!

THE 'CURL'
(PUBLIC URINAL
STANDING
ONLY)

BRIDGE

CANAL

RIGA AND
PRAGUE ARE
ALSO BIG STAG
DESTINATIONS

THE LAST
FREE NIGHT
OF THEIR LIFE!

MALE
DEER.

WHAT AN EXCUSE...

2ᴱ KAMER COFFEESHOP

IS ONE OF THE OLDER AND SMALLEST COFFEESHOPS IN AMSTERDAM'S CENTRE

2ᴱ KAMER IS DUTCH PARLIAMENT

OPEN 365 DAYS A YEAR FROM 10 AM TO 1 AM

IN AN ALLEY BETWEEN SPUI AND SINGEL

THIS RECEPTACLE CONTAINS THE ASHES OF AN AMERICAN REGULAR (DYING WISH)

NO CAPS ALLOWED! IT PUTS OFF CERTAIN CUSTOMERS AND IT'S A WAY OF DEMONSTRATI... AUTHORITY

IT CAN GET A BIT SMOKEY IN HERE (THEY OPEN THE FRONT DOOR)

AIRCO

SUPPLIER TO THE COURT? I THOUGHT THE KING DRANK BEER?

THIS ONE'S EMPTY

CAME...

COFF...

KA...

WATER PIPE (SPECIALLY FOR AMERICANS)

THIS IS A: MIRROR MAKES IT FEEL MORE SPACIOUS

OLD POSTER

SIGAREN Maestro

VLOEIBOX

SPIEGEL

FOTO VAN 'S MENS...

MUSIC LIST

BANK CARD MACHINE

READY ROLLED JOINTS

TEA

MILK

CIGARETTE PAPER VENDING MACHINE

TOURISTS ARE SMOKING A JOINT HERE A TEN IN THE MORNING, THEY JUST TOOK A PHOTO OF THE MENU. HOW LONG HAVE THEY BEEN IN AMSTERDAM?

COAT

BAG

A YOUNG WOMAN IS SITTING HERE

WHEN THEY WEIGH THE GRASS THE PRICE APPEARS ON THE SCREEN

PAPERS

25 TYPES OF GRASS AND 15 TYPES OF HASHISH... ISN'T THAT A BIT OVER THE TOP

TWO SCALES BECAUSE IT CAN GET BUSY HERE

EXTRA AIR

THEIR PLANE LANDED AT 7.28 THAT MORNING (A COUPLE OF HOURS)

IF YOU SMOKE EVERY DAY IT AFFECTS YOUR SHORT-TERM MEMORY... YOUR WHAT?

BETWEEN SITTING AND STANDING →

WHO SMOKES WHAT? YOUNG PEOPLE PREFER SKUNK (A SMACK IN THE FACE) OLDER WHITE SMOKE MEN SMOKE HASH (TO RELAX) TOURISTS GO FOR THE EXPENSIVE STUFF BECAUSE THEY THINK THAT'S THE BEST A POPULAR TYPE IS SUPERSILVERHAZE WICH GIVES AN ENERGETIC HIGH

STIMU-LATING

GRASS WITH LOTS OF THC

25% OF ALL TOURISTS WHO VISIT AMSTERDAM GO TO A COFFEESHOP (WHERE DO THE OTHERS GO?)

ALSO AVAILABLE WATERWORKS A THC CONCENTRATE AT 60 EURO'S A GRAM! (NOTHING SOFT ABOUT THAT)

ONLY FOR EXPERIENCED SMOKERS!

COFFEE SHOP

Production and distribution of marihuana is sanctioned by the government in Uruguay and recreational use of cannabis is legal in the US states of Washington and Colorado. Holland's big cities are planning to experiment with legalised cultivation of the crop.

VER
TI

Drawing Amsterdam the way I have for all these years, I have seen how things are always changing. Just as water finds its own level, a city like Amsterdam is constantly adjusting to new circumstances.

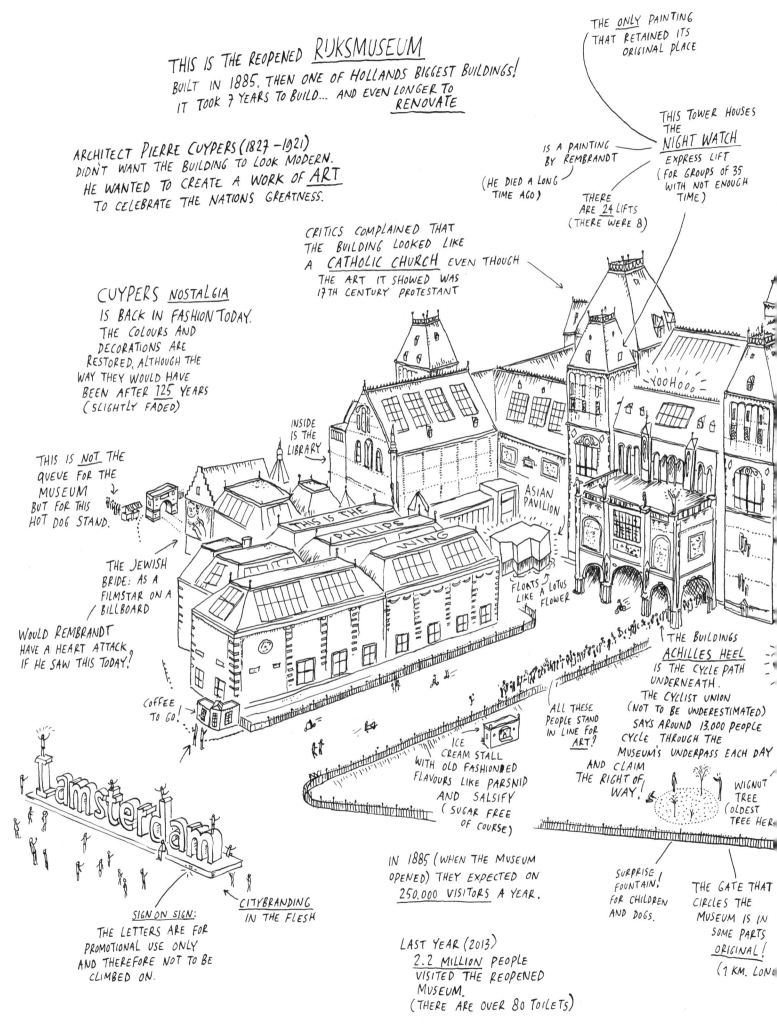

THIS IS THE REOPENED **RIJKSMUSEUM**
BUILT IN 1885, THEN ONE OF HOLLANDS BIGGEST BUILDINGS!
IT TOOK 7 YEARS TO BUILD... AND EVEN LONGER TO RENOVATE

ARCHITECT PIERRE CUYPERS (1827–1921) DIDN'T WANT THE BUILDING TO LOOK MODERN. HE WANTED TO CREATE A WORK OF **ART** TO CELEBRATE THE NATIONS GREATNESS.

CUYPERS **NOSTALGIA** IS BACK IN FASHION TODAY. THE COLOURS AND DECORATIONS ARE RESTORED, ALTHOUGH THE WAY THEY WOULD HAVE BEEN AFTER 125 YEARS (SLIGHTLY FADED)

THIS IS **NOT** THE QUEUE FOR THE MUSEUM BUT FOR THIS HOT DOG STAND.

THE JEWISH BRIDE: AS A FILMSTAR ON A BILLBOARD

WOULD REMBRANDT HAVE A HEART ATTACK IF HE SAW THIS TODAY?

COFFEE TO GO!

CRITICS COMPLAINED THAT THE BUILDING LOOKED LIKE A **CATHOLIC CHURCH** EVEN THOUGH THE ART IT SHOWED WAS 17TH CENTURY PROTESTANT

INSIDE IS THE LIBRARY

THE **ONLY** PAINTING THAT RETAINED ITS ORIGINAL PLACE

THIS TOWER HOUSES THE **NIGHT WATCH** EXPRESS LIFT (FOR GROUPS OF 35 WITH NOT ENOUGH TIME)

IS A PAINTING BY REMBRANDT

(HE DIED A LONG TIME AGO)

THERE ARE 24 LIFTS (THERE WERE 8)

YOOHOOO

ASIAN PAVILION

THIS IS THE PHILIPS WING

FLOATS LIKE A LOTUS FLOWER

THE BUILDINGS **ACHILLES HEEL** IS THE CYCLE PATH UNDERNEATH. THE CYCLIST UNION (NOT TO BE UNDERESTIMATED) SAYS AROUND 13.000 PEOPLE CYCLE THROUGH THE MUSEUM'S UNDERPASS EACH DAY AND CLAIM THE RIGHT OF WAY.

ALL THESE PEOPLE STAND IN LINE FOR ART?

ICE CREAM STALL WITH OLD FASHIONED FLAVOURS LIKE PARSNIP AND SALSIFY (SUGAR FREE OF COURSE)

WIGNUT TREE (OLDEST TREE HER...

SURPRISE FOUNTAIN! FOR CHILDREN AND DOGS.

THE GATE THAT CIRCLES THE MUSEUM IS IN SOME PARTS **ORIGINAL**! (1 KM. LON...

I amsterdam

SIGN ON SIGN: THE LETTERS ARE FOR PROMOTIONAL USE ONLY AND THEREFORE NOT TO BE CLIMBED ON.

CITYBRANDING IN THE FLESH

IN 1885 (WHEN THE MUSEUM OPENED) THEY EXPECTED ON 250.000 VISITORS A YEAR.

LAST YEAR (2013) 2.2 MILLION PEOPLE VISITED THE REOPENED MUSEUM. (THERE ARE OVER 80 TOILETS)

RIJKSMUSEUM

In 2004, Amsterdam launched the 'I Amsterdam' city brand to attract expats, tourists and foreign investors to the city. The huge 'I Amsterdam' sign in front of the Rijksmuseum is now one of the city's most photographed objects.

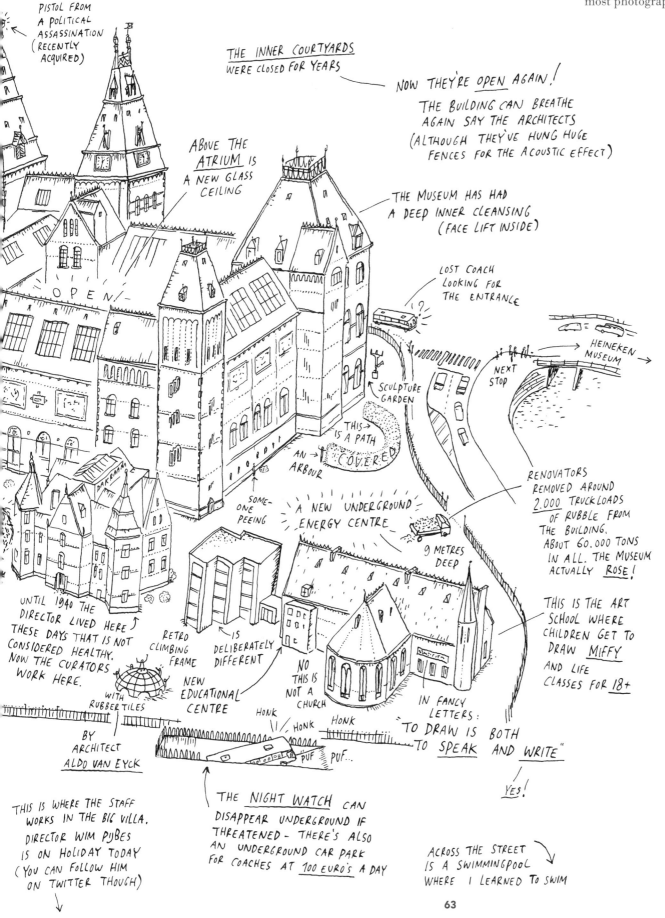

PISTOL FROM A POLITICAL ASSASSINATION (RECENTLY ACQUIRED)

THE INNER COURTYARDS WERE CLOSED FOR YEARS

NOW THEY'RE OPEN AGAIN!
THE BUILDING CAN BREATHE AGAIN SAY THE ARCHITECTS (ALTHOUGH THEY'VE HUNG HUGE FENCES FOR THE ACOUSTIC EFFECT)

ABOVE THE ATRIUM IS A NEW GLASS CEILING

THE MUSEUM HAS HAD A DEEP INNER CLEANSING (FACE LIFT INSIDE)

LOST COACH LOOKING FOR THE ENTRANCE

HEINEKEN MUSEUM →

NEXT STOP

SCULPTURE GARDEN

THIS → IS A PATH

COVERED

AN → ARBOUR

RENOVATORS REMOVED AROUND 2.000 TRUCKLOADS OF RUBBLE FROM THE BUILDING, ABOUT 60.000 TONS IN ALL. THE MUSEUM ACTUALLY ROSE!

SOME- ONE PEEING

A NEW UNDERGROUND ENERGY CENTRE

9 METRES DEEP

UNTIL 1940 THE DIRECTOR LIVED HERE ↑ THESE DAYS THAT IS NOT CONSIDERED HEALTHY. NOW THE CURATORS WORK HERE.

RETRO CLIMBING FRAME

→ IS DELIBERATELY DIFFERENT

NEW EDUCATIONAL CENTRE

NO THIS IS NOT A CHURCH

THIS IS THE ART SCHOOL WHERE CHILDREN GET TO DRAW MIFFY AND LIFE CLASSES FOR 18+

WITH RUBBER TILES

IN FANCY LETTERS: "TO DRAW IS BOTH TO SPEAK AND WRITE"

HONK

HONK HONK

BY ARCHITECT ALDO VAN EYCK

PUF PUF...

YES!

THIS IS WHERE THE STAFF WORKS IN THE BIG VILLA. DIRECTOR WIM PIJBES IS ON HOLIDAY TODAY (YOU CAN FOLLOW HIM ON TWITTER THOUGH) ↓

THE NIGHT WATCH CAN DISAPPEAR UNDERGROUND IF THREATENED - THERE'S ALSO AN UNDERGROUND CAR PARK FOR COACHES AT 100 EURO'S A DAY

ACROSS THE STREET IS A SWIMMINGPOOL WHERE I LEARNED TO SWIM

CIRCUMCISION CENTRE

Since a German judge decided that circumcising boys without a medical reason was a crime, a campaign has started in Holland to ban circumcising boys aged under 12. Dutch medical organisations oppose a prohibition, arguing that the procedure would then be done illegally.

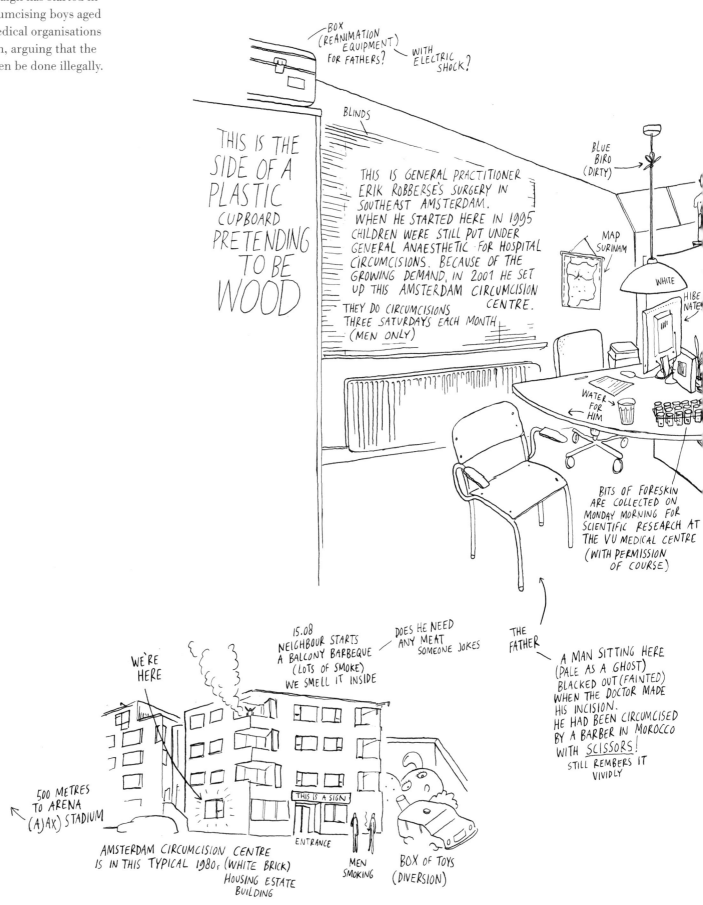

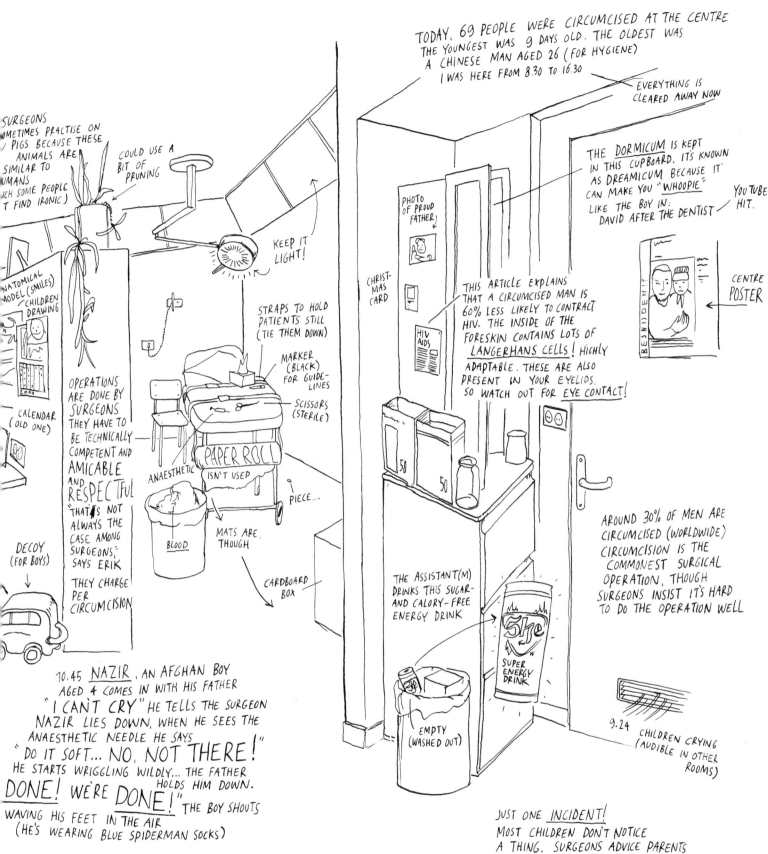

TODAY, 69 PEOPLE WERE CIRCUMCISED AT THE CENTRE THE YOUNGEST WAS 9 DAYS OLD. THE OLDEST WAS A CHINESE MAN AGED 26 (FOR HYGIENE) I WAS HERE FROM 8.30 TO 16.30

EVERYTHING IS CLEARED AWAY NOW

SURGEONS SOMETIMES PRACTISE ON PIGS BECAUSE THESE ANIMALS ARE SIMILAR TO HUMANS (WHICH SOME PEOPLE MIGHT FIND IRONIC)

COULD USE A BIT OF PRUNING

KEEP IT LIGHT!

THE DORMICUM IS KEPT IN THIS CUPBOARD. IT'S KNOWN AS DREAMICUM BECAUSE IT CAN MAKE YOU "WHOOPIE" LIKE THE BOY IN: DAVID AFTER THE DENTIST

YOU TUBE HIT.

PHOTO OF PROUD FATHER

CHRIST-MAS CARD

THIS ARTICLE EXPLAINS THAT A CIRCUMCISED MAN IS 60% LESS LIKELY TO CONTRACT HIV. THE INSIDE OF THE FORESKIN CONTAINS LOTS OF LANGERHANS CELLS! HIGHLY ADAPTABLE. THESE ARE ALSO PRESENT IN YOUR EYELIDS. SO WATCH OUT FOR EYE CONTACT!

CENTRE POSTER

BESNIJDENIS

ANATOMICAL MODEL (SMILES)
CHILDREN DRAWING

OPERATIONS ARE DONE BY SURGEONS THEY HAVE TO BE TECHNICALLY COMPETENT AND AMICABLE AND RESPECTFUL "THAT'S NOT ALWAYS THE CASE AMONG SURGEONS" SAYS ERIK THEY CHARGE PER CIRCUMCISION

CALENDAR (OLD ONE)

STRAPS TO HOLD PATIENTS STILL (TIE THEM DOWN)

MARKER (BLACK) FOR GUIDE-LINES

SCISSORS (STERILE)

PAPER ROLL ISN'T USED

ANAESTHETIC

PIECE...

BLOOD

MATS ARE THOUGH

DECOY (FOR BOYS)

CARDBOARD BOX

THE ASSISTANT(M) DRINKS THIS SUGAR- AND CALORY-FREE ENERGY DRINK

She SUPER ENERGY DRINK

AROUND 30% OF MEN ARE CIRCUMCISED (WORLDWIDE) CIRCUMCISION IS THE COMMONEST SURGICAL OPERATION. THOUGH SURGEONS INSIST IT'S HARD TO DO THE OPERATION WELL

EMPTY (WASHED OUT)

9.24 CHILDREN CRYING (AUDIBLE IN OTHER ROOMS)

10.45 NAZIR, AN AFGHAN BOY AGED 4 COMES IN WITH HIS FATHER "I CAN'T CRY" HE TELLS THE SURGEON NAZIR LIES DOWN, WHEN HE SEES THE ANAESTHETIC NEEDLE HE SAYS "DO IT SOFT... NO, NOT THERE!" HE STARTS WRIGGLING WILDLY... THE FATHER HOLDS HIM DOWN. "DONE! WE'RE DONE!" THE BOY SHOUTS WAVING HIS FEET IN THE AIR (HE'S WEARING BLUE SPIDERMAN SOCKS)

I CAN'T WORK LIKE THIS THE SURGEON SIGHS AND GIVES HIM A DORMICUM SUPPOSITORY MINUTES LATER NAZIR IS FLOPPING ABOUT LIKE HE'S MADE OF RUBBER. THE FATHER SAYS "CHICK CHAK AND THEN LOADS OF PRESENTS" "PLAY STATION 2?" ASKS THE BOY. "WHAT ELSE," REPLIES THE FATHER "PLAY STATION 1?" NAZIR SLURS WITH A THICKENING TONGUE.

JUST ONE INCIDENT! MOST CHILDREN DON'T NOTICE A THING. SURGEONS ADVICE PARENTS TO CIRCUMCISE EITHER IN THE FIRST YEAR OR AFTER A CHILD TURNS 5. THEN THEY CAN UNDERSTAND AND DO WHAT THEY'RE TOLD! (LESS FEAR)

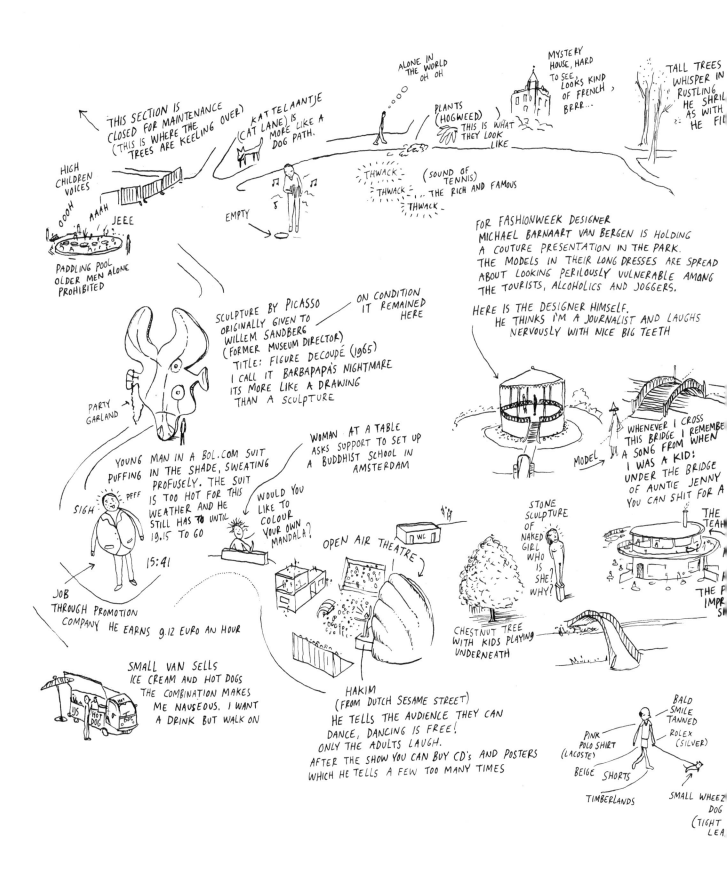

VONDEL PARK

The Vondelpark is designed as an English landscape, giving park enthusiasts the sense of being out in the country. Perhaps that explains the 350,000 kilos of trash people leave behind. Do they imagine they are in the middle of nowhere and no one will notice?

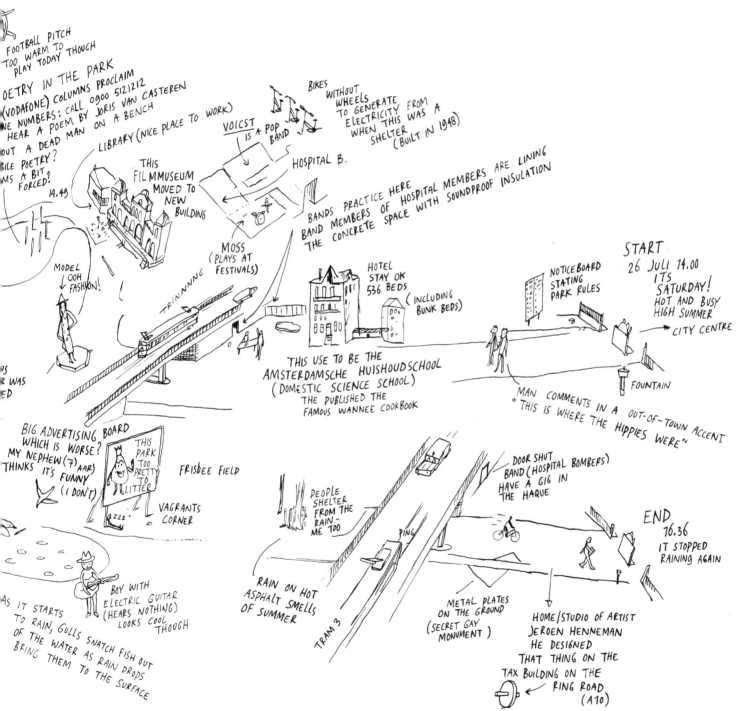

EZE
HILD,
WIND
SALIS
← DUTCH POET

FOOTBALL PITCH TOO WARM TO PLAY TODAY THOUGH

OETRY IN THE PARK
(VODAFONE) COLUMNS PROCLAIM NE NUMBERS: CALL 0900 5121212 HEAR A POEM BY JORIS VAN CASTEREN OUT A DEAD MAN ON A BENCH ILE POETRY? MS A BIT FORCED!
14.49

LIBRARY (NICE PLACE TO WORK)

VOICST IS A POP BAND

BIKES WITHOUT WHEELS TO GENERATE ELECTRICITY FROM WHEN THIS WAS A SHELTER (BUILT IN 1948)

THIS FILMMUSEUM MOVED TO NEW BUILDING

HOSPITAL B.

BANDS PRACTICE HERE
BAND MEMBERS OF HOSPITAL MEMBERS ARE LINING THE CONCRETE SPACE WITH SOUNDPROOF INSULATION

MODEL OOH FASHION!

MOSS (PLAYS AT FESTIVALS)

TRINNING

HOTEL STAY OK 536 BEDS (INCLUDING BUNK BEDS)

NOTICEBOARD STATING PARK RULES

START 26 JULI 14.00 ITS SATURDAY! HOT AND BUSY HIGH SUMMER
→ CITY CENTRE

PS R WAS ED

THIS USE TO BE THE AMSTERDAMSCHE HUISHOUDSCHOOL (DOMESTIC SCIENCE SCHOOL) THE PUBLISHED THE FAMOUS WANNEE COOKBOOK

FOUNTAIN

MAN COMMENTS IN A OUT-OF-TOWN ACCENT "THIS IS WHERE THE HIPPIES WERE"

BIG ADVERTISING BOARD WHICH IS WORSE? MY NEPHEW (7) AAR) THINKS IT'S FUNNY (I DON'T)

THIS PARK TOO PRETTY TO LITTER

FRISBEE FIELD

VAGRANTS CORNER

PEOPLE SHELTER FROM THE RAIN - ME TOO

PING

DOOR SHUT BAND (HOSPITAL BOMBERS) HAVE A GIG IN THE HAQUE

END 16.36 IT STOPPED RAINING AGAIN

AS IT STARTS TO RAIN, GULLS SNATCH FISH OUT OF THE WATER AS RAIN DROPS BRING THEM TO THE SURFACE

BOY WITH ELECTRIC GUITAR (HEARS NOTHING) LOOKS COOL THOUGH

RAIN ON HOT ASPHALT SMELLS OF SUMMER

TRAM 3

METAL PLATES ON THE GROUND (SECRET GAY MONUMENT)

HOME/STUDIO OF ARTIST JEROEN HENNEMAN HE DESIGNED THAT THING ON THE TAX BUILDING ON THE RING ROAD (A10)

BOOKSHOP

With one bookshop for every 6,500 people, the city has the biggest concentration in a country with more bookshops per head than any other. Yet numbers have declined since 2007. These days, online bookshops, supermarkets, gas stations and department stores all sell books.

FRENCH LITERATURE

BOVARY

PEREC

POETRY = FOR THOSE WHO LOVE FRENCH

TURKISH LANGUAGE BOOKS (MAINLY PURCHASED BY PRISON LIBRARIES PEOPLE READ TURKISH THERE

THESE WALLS

IN BETWEEN IS A NARROW STAIRCASE

THE ORACLE →

A FAMOUS (BIG) FOOD CRITIC LIVES UPSTAIRS

IT IS QUIET HERE AND AIR IS DRIER...

DRAWING OF WIARDA

FOREIGN LANGUAGES AREN'T STRANGE HERE!

IN THE WINDOW ARE THE NEW POETRY BOOKS. THE PAGES CURL UP IN THE SUN 500 POEMS EVERYBODY HAS TO HAVE READ! (I DON'T HAVE TO DO ANY-THING!)

THIS LEADS DOWN TO THE FOSSILISED LANGUAGES GREEK AND LATIN

POETRY CORNER

MAP OF ANCIENT WORLD

ATLASES ARE STORED UNDER THE COMPUTER (STAFF ONLY)

THIS IS THE NEWS CENTRE

MAGAZINES FROM SOUTH AFRICA

AT THE CASH REGISTER IS PETRA SHE THINKS OTHER PEOPLE THINK SHE'S A BITCH (SHE ISN'T OF COURSE) ALL KINDS OF PEOPLE COME HERE ALTHOUGH THERE ARE NOT MANY MORROCAN AND TURKISH NEWSPAPERS AND MAGAZINES

FASHION

GLAMOUR AIR

UNDER-NEATH POETRY ANTHO-LOGIES (WELL HIDDEN)

LITERARY THEORY

ONE LEVEL DOWN: COOKERY BOOKS; ALSO PECULIAR BOOKS

TRAVEL GUIDES

POST-CARDS

THIS IS THE BEAUTIFUL PEOPLE'S CORNER WHO DO NOT READ BUT LOOK AT PICS OF PRETTY PEOPLE!

TOURIST MAPS

"THE GREEN" AMSTERDAMMER WEEKLY MAGA-ZINE IS SELLING WELL

DESIGN IS DOWN

TRAVELGUIDES ARE A MASSIVE MARKET! THEY USED TO HAVE BOOKS ABOUT POP MUSIC A SHRINKING MARKET (POOR MUSICIANS...)

POP MUSIC

DESK FOR ORDERS

UP → CASH REGISTER

HERE WE READ ENGLISH PLEASE

BO WRIT

PIN →

WINDOW

NO THRESHOLD! THATS FOR NEXT DOOR →

DARKBLUE WOODEN CRATES

HERE ONE FINDS ALL SORTS OF ALTERNATIVE PUBLICATIONS ALSO KNOWN AS THE STAPLE PROLETARIAT! FOR THE REVOLUTIONARIES AMONG US.

15:48 PM I SEE A FORMERLY FAMOUS TV PRESENTER... (FACE IS WRINKLED LIKE PAPER)

16:07 PM WELL KNOWN WRITER BOUAZZA BUYS A NEWS-PAPER SOBER

HERE

(YOU OR I) THE CHANCES OF MEETING SOMEONE YOU (OR I) KNOW ARE VERY GOOD! "HEY HOW ARE YOU..."

LEIPE SHIT OUWE (LOOSELY TRANSLATED) "CRAZY SHIT OLD MAN"

SCULPTURE OF LITTLE RASCAL WITH A SMALL GOLDEN HEA HAR

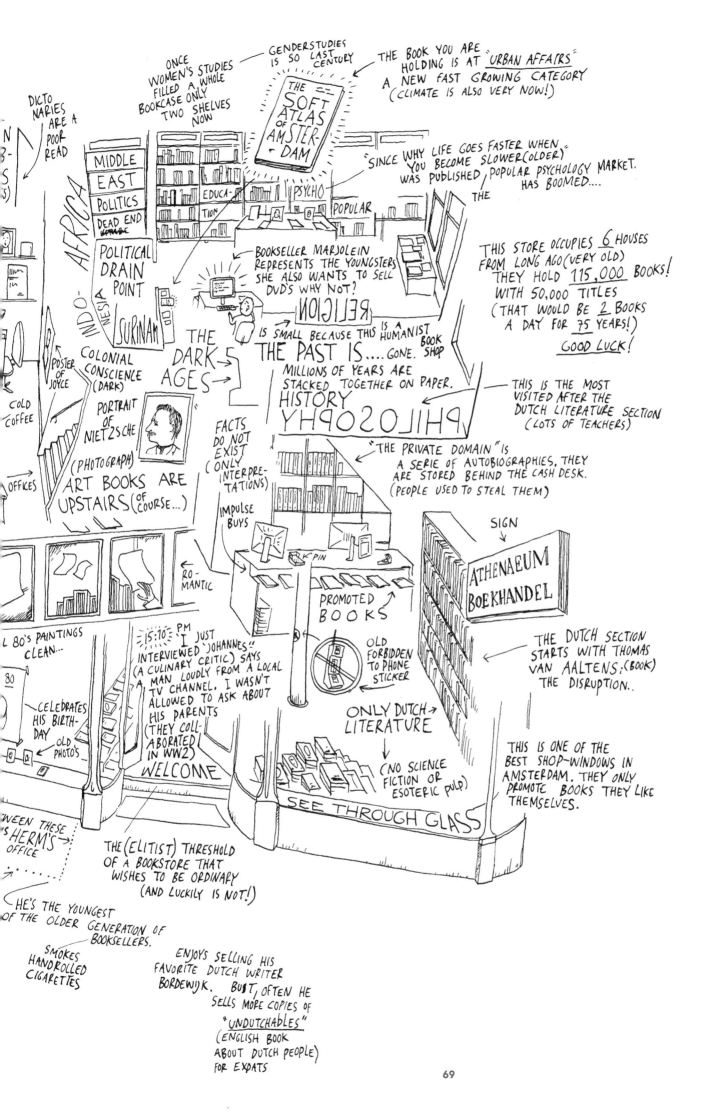

ONCE WOMEN'S STUDIES FILLED A WHOLE BOOKCASE ONLY TWO SHELVES NOW

GENDERSTUDIES IS SO LAST CENTURY

THE BOOK YOU ARE HOLDING IS AT "URBAN AFFAIRS" A NEW FAST GROWING CATEGORY (CLIMATE IS ALSO VERY NOW!)

DICTIONARIES ARE A POOR READ

N B-S (S)

MIDDLE EAST POLITICS DEAD END

AFRICA

EDUCA-TION

PSYCHO

POPULAR

THE SOFT ATLAS OF AMSTER-DAM

SINCE WHY WAS PUBLISHED

LIFE GOES FASTER WHEN YOU BECOME SLOWER (OLDER) POPULAR PSYCHOLOGY MARKET HAS BOOMED....

THE

POLITICAL DRAIN POINT

INDO-NESIA SURINAM

BOOKSELLER MARJOLEIN REPRESENTS THE YOUNGSTERS SHE ALSO WANTS TO SELL DVD'S WHY NOT?

RELIGION

IS SMALL BECAUSE THIS IS A HUMANIST BOOK SHOP

THIS STORE OCCUPIES 6 HOUSES FROM LONG AGO (VERY OLD) THEY HOLD 115,000 BOOKS! WITH 50,000 TITLES (THAT WOULD BE 2 BOOKS A DAY FOR 75 YEARS!) GOOD LUCK!

THE DARK 5 AGES →

THE PAST IS.... GONE. MILLIONS OF YEARS ARE STACKED TOGETHER ON PAPER.

HISTORY PHILOSOPHY

THIS IS THE MOST VISITED AFTER THE DUTCH LITERATURE SECTION (LOTS OF TEACHERS)

POSTER OF JOYCE

COLONIAL CONSCIENCE (DARK)

PORTRAIT OF NIETZSCHE

COLD COFFEE

FACTS DO NOT EXIST (ONLY INTERPRE-TATIONS)

(PHOTOGRAPH) ART BOOKS ARE UPSTAIRS (OF COURSE...)

"THE PRIVATE DOMAIN" IS A SERIE OF AUTOBIOGRAPHIES, THEY ARE STORED BEHIND THE CASH DESK. (PEOPLE USED TO STEAL THEM)

OFFICES

IMPULSE BUYS

SIGN

ATHENAEUM BOEKHANDEL

RO-MANTIC

L 80's PAINTINGS CLEAN...

80

PROMOTED BOOKS

OLD FORBIDDEN TO PHONE STICKER

THE DUTCH SECTION STARTS WITH THOMAS VAN AALTENS: (BOOK) THE DISRUPTION..

15:10 PM I JUST INTERVIEWED "JOHANNES" (A CULINARY CRITIC) SAYS A MAN LOUDLY FROM A LOCAL TV CHANNEL. I WASN'T ALLOWED TO ASK ABOUT HIS PARENTS (THEY COLL-ABORATED IN WW2)

CELEBRATES HIS BIRTH-DAY OLD PHOTO'S

WELCOME

ONLY DUTCH LITERATURE

(NO SCIENCE FICTION OR ESOTERIC PULP)

THIS IS ONE OF THE BEST SHOP-WINDOWS IN AMSTERDAM. THEY ONLY PROMOTE BOOKS THEY LIKE THEMSELVES.

WEEN THESE 'S HERM'S → OFFICE

SEE THROUGH GLASS

THE (ELITIST) THRESHOLD OF A BOOKSTORE THAT WISHES TO BE ORDINARY (AND LUCKILY IS NOT!)

HE'S THE YOUNGEST OF THE OLDER GENERATION OF BOOKSELLERS.

SMOKES HANDROLLED CIGARETTES

ENJOYS SELLING HIS FAVORITE DUTCH WRITER BORDEWIJK. BUT, OFTEN HE SELLS MORE COPIES OF "UNDUTCHABLES" (ENGLISH BOOK ABOUT DUTCH PEOPLE) FOR EXPATS

SHOPPING STREETS

The local shops came up with a name for their neighbourhood: the Nine Streets. It was so successful that many can no longer afford the rising rents and the big chains are moving in.

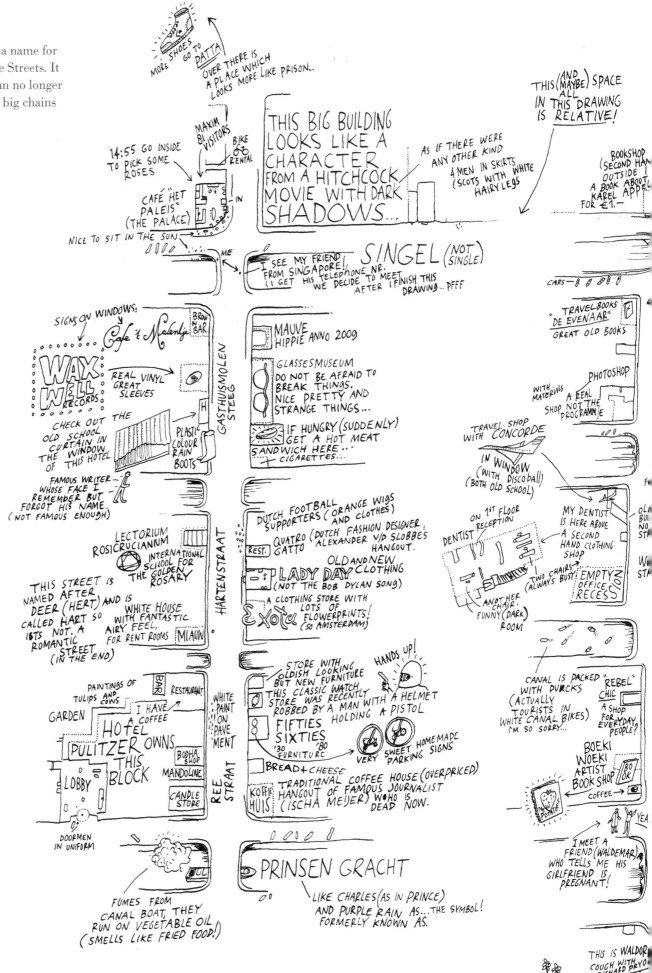

MORE SHOES GO TO PATTA

OVER THERE IS A PLACE WHICH LOOKS MORE LIKE PRISON..

THIS (AND MAYBE) ALL SPACE IN THIS DRAWING IS RELATIVE!

14:55 GO INSIDE TO PICK SOME ROSES

MAXIM 81 VISITORS

BIKE RENTAL

THIS BIG BUILDING LOOKS LIKE A CHARACTER FROM A HITCHCOCK MOVIE WITH DARK SHADOWS...

AS IF THERE WERE ANY OTHER KIND 4 MEN IN SKIRTS (SCOTS WITH WHITE HAIRY LEGS

BOOKSHOP (SECOND HAN OUTSIDE A BOOK ABOUT KAREL APPE FOR €1.—

CAFÉ "HET PALEIS" (THE PALACE)

IN

NICE TO SIT IN THE SUN

ME

I SEE MY FRIEND FROM SINGAPORE! (I GET HIS TELEPHONE NR. WE DECIDE TO MEET AFTER I FINISH THIS DRAWING.. PFFF

SINGEL (NOT SINGLE)

CARS—

TRAVEL BOOKS DE EVENAAR GREAT OLD BOOKS

SIGNS ON WINDOWS:

Café 't Molentje

BROW N BAR

WAX WELL RECORDS

REAL VINYL GREAT SLEEVES

CHECK OUT THE OLD SCHOOL CURTAIN IN THE WINDOW OF THIS HOTEL

PLASTIC COLOUR RAIN BOOTS

GASTHUISMOLEN STEEG

H

MAUVE HIPPIE ANNO 2009

GLASSESMUSEUM DO NOT BE AFRAID TO BREAK THINGS. NICE PRETTY AND STRANGE THINGS...

IF HUNGRY (SUDDENLY) GET A HOT MEAT SANDWICH HERE .. CIGARETTES...

WITH MATERIALS

A REAL SHOP NOT THE PROGRAMME

PHOTOSHOP

TRAVEL SHOP WITH CONCORDE

IN WINDOW (WITH DISCO ball) (BOTH OLD SCHOOL)

ON 1ST FLOOR DENTIST RECEPTION

MY DENTIST IS HERE ABOVE A SECOND HAND CLOTHING SHOP

OL BUI NO STR

FAMOUS WRITER WHOSE FACE I REMEMBER BUT FORGOT HIS NAME (NOT FAMOUS ENOUGH)

LECTORIUM ROSICRUCIANUM

INTERNATIONAL SCHOOL FOR THE GOLDEN ROSARY

HARTENSTRAAT

DUTCH FOOTBALL SUPPORTERS (ORANGE WIGS AND CLOTHES)

REST. QUATRO GATTO (DUTCH FASHION DESIGNER ALEXANDER V/D SLOBBES HANGOUT.

OLD AND NEW CLOTHING

LADY DAY (NOT THE BOB DYLAN SONG)

TWO CHAIRS (ALWAYS BUSY)

EMPTY OFFICE RECESSION

THIS STREET IS NAMED AFTER DEER (HERT) AND IS CALLED HART SO IS IT NOT A ROMANTIC STREET (IN THE END)

WHITE HOUSE WITH FANTASTIC AIRY FEEL, FOR RENT ROOMS

MIAUW

A CLOTHING STORE WITH LOTS OF FLOWERPRINTS! (SO AMSTERDAM)

Exota

ANOTHER CHAIR FUNNY (DARK) ROOM

CANAL IS PACKED WITH DUTCKS (ACTUALLY TOURISTS IN WHITE CANAL BIKES) I'M SO SORRY...

"REBEL" CHIC A SHOP FOR EVERYDAY PEOPLE?

W STR

PAINTINGS OF TULIPS AND COWS

GARDEN

BAR

RESTAURANT

I HAVE A COFFEE

HOTEL PULITZER OWNS THIS BLOCK

LOBBY

BUDHA SHOP

MANDOLINE

CANDLE STORE

WHITE PAINT ON PAVE MENT

REE STRAAT

STORE WITH OLDISH LOOKING BUT NEW FURNITURE THIS CLASSIC WATCH STORE WAS RECENTLY ROBBED BY A MAN WITH A HELMET HOLDING A PISTOL

HANDS UP!

FIFTIES SIXTIES '30 '80 FURNITURE

VERY SWEET HOMEMADE PARKING SIGNS

BREAD + CHEESE

KOFFIE HUIS

TRADITIONAL COFFEE HOUSE (OVERPRICED) HANGOUT OF FAMOUS JOURNALIST (ISCHA MEIJER) WHO IS DEAD NOW.

BOEKI WOEKI ARTIST BOOK SHOP

BO OK

COFFEE

I MEET A FRIEND (WALDEMAR) WHO TELLS ME HIS GIRLFRIEND IS PREGNANT!

YEA

DOORMEN IN UNIFORM

FUMES FROM CANAL BOAT, THEY RUN ON VEGETABLE OIL (SMELLS LIKE FRIED FOOD!)

PRINSEN GRACHT

LIKE CHARLES (AS IN PRINCE) AND PURPLE RAIN AS...THE SYMBOL! FORMERLY KNOWN AS.

THIS IS WALDOR COUGH WITH RICHARD PRYO

REAL FLOWERS IN ORANGINA BOTTLE ON TABLE

BIG ROUND WALL PICTURE OF CASTLE

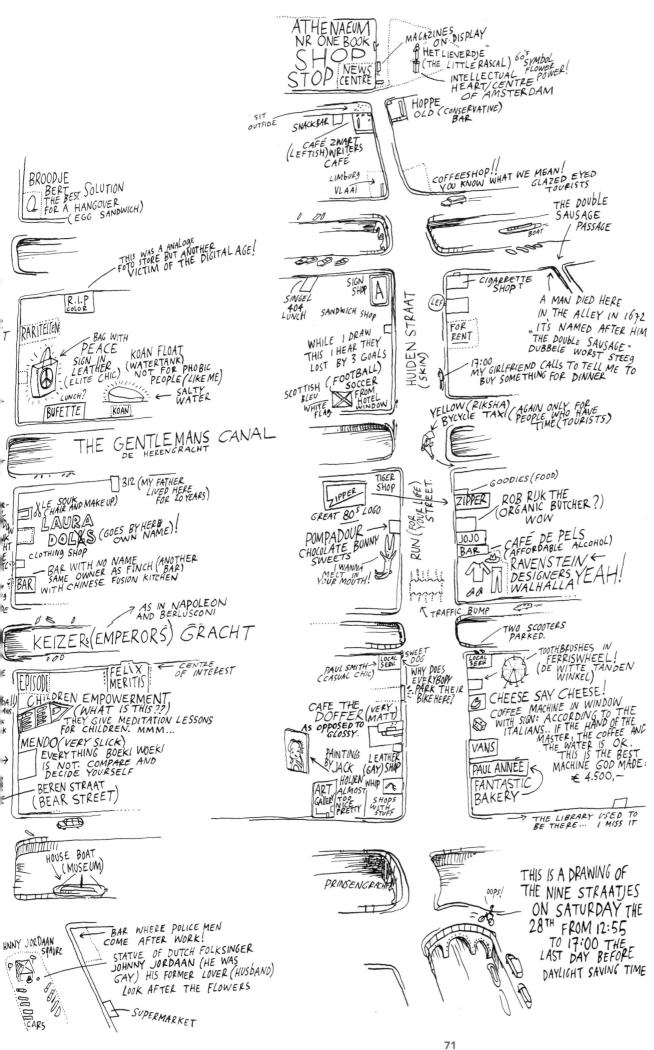

ATHENAEUM NR ONE BOOK SHOP STOP NEWS CENTRE

MAGAZINES ON DISPLAY

"HET LIEVERDJE" (THE LITTLE RASCAL) 60's SYMBOL FLOWER POWER!

INTELLECTUAL HEART/CENTRE OF AMSTERDAM

HOPPE OLD (CONSERVATIVE) BAR

SIT OUTSIDE

SNACKBAR

CAFÉ ZWART (LEFTISH) WRITERS CAFE

LIMBURG VLAAI

COFFEESHOP!! YOU KNOW WHAT WE MEAN! GLAZED EYED TOURISTS

THE DOUBLE SAUSAGE PASSAGE

BOAT

BROODJE BERT the BEST Solution FOR A HANGOVER (EGG SANDWICH)

THIS WAS A ANALOGE FOTO STORE BUT ANOTHER VICTIM OF THE DIGITAL AGE!

R.I.P. COLOR

RÄRITEITEN

BAG WITH PEACE SIGN IN LEATHER (ELITE CHIC)

KOAN FLOAT (WATERTANK) NOT FOR PHOBIC PEOPLE (LIKE ME)

SALTY ← WATER

LUNCH?

BUFETTE   KOAN

SINGEL 404 LUNCH

SIGN SHOP A

SANDWICH SHOP

WHILE I DRAW THIS I HEAR THEY LOST BY 3 GOALS

SCOTTISH BLEU (FOOTBALL) SOCCER FROM HOTEL WINDOW

WHITE FLAG

HUIDEN STRAAT (SKIN)

LEF

CIGARRETTE SHOP

FOR RENT

A MAN DIED HERE IN THE ALLEY IN 1672 "ITS NAMED AFTER HIM THE DOUBLE SAUSAGE · DUBBELE WORST STEEG

17:00 MY GIRLFRIEND CALLS TO TELL ME TO BUY SOMETHING FOR DINNER

YELLOW (RIKSHA) BYCICLE TAXI (AGAIN ONLY FOR PEOPLE WHO HAVE TIME (TOURISTS)

THE GENTLEMANS CANAL
DE HERENGRACHT

312 (MY FATHER LIVED HERE FOR 20 YEARS)

X LE SOUK (CHAIR AND MAKE UP)

LAURA DOLS (GOES BY HER OWN NAME)!

CLOTHING SHOP

BAR WITH NO NAME SAME OWNER AS FINCH (ANOTHER BAR) WITH CHINESE FUSION KITCHEN

BAR

ZIPPER

GREAT 80s LOGO

POMPADOUR CHOCOLATE BUNNY SWEETS

I WANNA MELT IN YOUR MOUTH!

TIGER SHOP

RUN (FOR YOUR LIFE) STREET.

GOODIES (FOOD)

ZIPPER

ROB RIJK THE (ORGANIC BUTCHER?) WOW

JOJO BAR

CAFÉ DE PELS (AFFORDABLE ALCOHOL)

RAVENSTEIN ← DESIGNERS YEAH! WALHALLA

TRAFFIC BUMP

KEIZERs (EMPERORS) GRACHT

AS IN NAPOLEON AND BERLUSCONI

FELIX MERITIS

CENTRE OF INTEREST

EPISODE

CHILDREN EMPOWERMENT (WHAT IS THIS ??) THEY GIVE MEDITATION LESSONS FOR CHILDREN. MMM...

MENDO (VERY SLICK) EVERYTHING BOEKI WOEKI IS NOT. COMPARE AND DECIDE YOURSELF

BEREN STRAAT (BEAR STREET)

PAUL SMITH (CASUAL CHIC)

LOCAL SERV.

SWEET DOG

WHY DOES EVERYBODY PARK THEIR BIKE HERE?

CAFE THE DOFFER AS OPPOSED TO GLOSSY.

(VERY MATT)

PAINTINGS BY JACK

LEATHER (GAY) SHOP

ART GALLERY

HOLDEN ALMOST TOO NICE PRETTY

WHIP

SHOPS WITH STUFF

TWO SCOOTERS PARKED.

LOCAL SERV.

TOOTHBRUSHES IN FERRISWHEEL! (DE WITTE TANDEN WINKEL)

CHEESE SAY CHEESE! COFFEE MACHINE IN WINDOW WITH SIGN: ACCORDING TO THE ITALIANS.. IF THE HAND OF THE MASTER, THE COFFEE AND THE WATER IS OK. THIS IS THE BEST MACHINE GOD MADE: € 4.500,—

VANS

PAUL ANNÉE

FANTASTIC BAKERY

THE LIBRARY USED TO BE THERE... I MISS IT

HOUSE BOAT (MUSEUM)

PRINSENGRACHT

OOPS!

THIS IS A DRAWING OF THE NINE STRAATJES ON SATURDAY THE 28TH FROM 12:55 TO 17:00 THE LAST DAY BEFORE DAYLIGHT SAVING TIME

HNNY JORDAAN SRAURE

BAR WHERE POLICE MEN COME AFTER WORK!

STATUE OF DUTCH FOLKSINGER JOHNNY JORDAAN (HE WAS GAY) HIS FORMER LOVER (HUSBAND) LOOK AFTER THE FLOWERS

CARS

SUPERMARKET

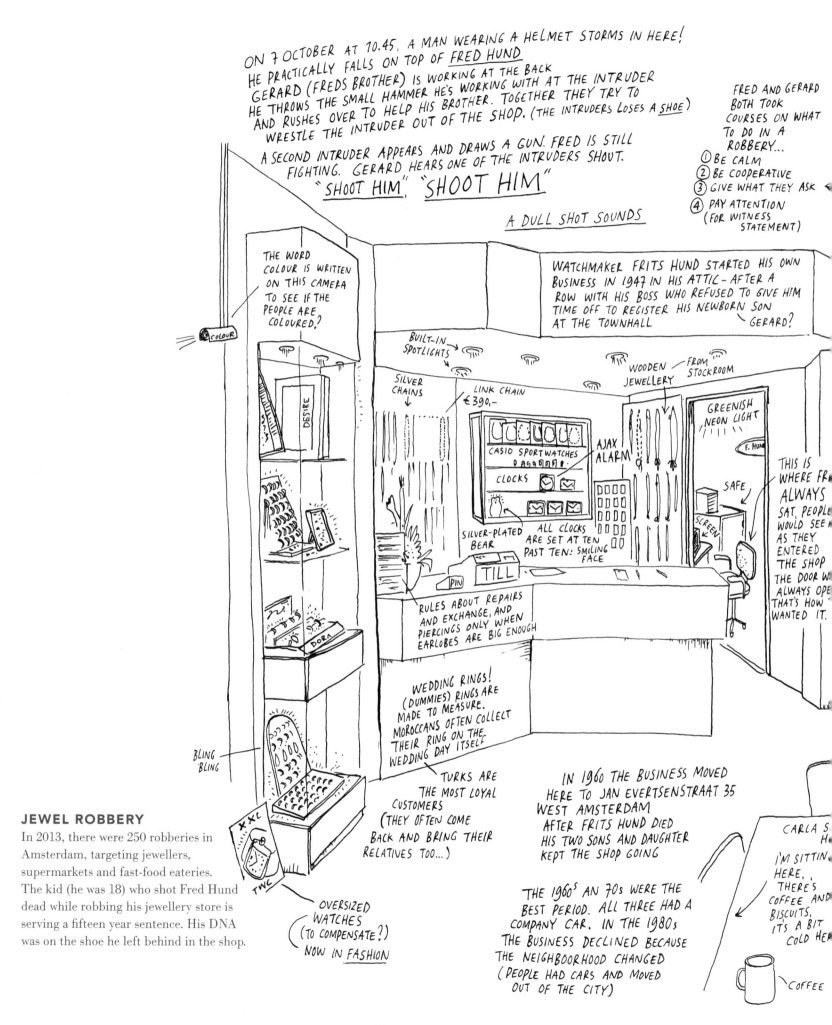

ON 7 OCTOBER AT 10.45, A MAN WEARING A HELMET STORMS IN HERE!
HE PRACTICALLY FALLS ON TOP OF FRED HUND
GERARD (FREDS BROTHER) IS WORKING AT THE BACK
HE THROWS THE SMALL HAMMER HE'S WORKING WITH AT THE INTRUDER
AND RUSHES OVER TO HELP HIS BROTHER. TOGETHER THEY TRY TO
WRESTLE THE INTRUDER OUT OF THE SHOP. (THE INTRUDERS LOSES A SHOE)

A SECOND INTRUDER APPEARS AND DRAWS A GUN. FRED IS STILL
FIGHTING. GERARD HEARS ONE OF THE INTRUDERS SHOUT.
"SHOOT HIM", "SHOOT HIM"

A DULL SHOT SOUNDS

FRED AND GERARD
BOTH TOOK
COURSES ON WHAT
TO DO IN A
ROBBERY...
① BE CALM
② BE COOPERATIVE
③ GIVE WHAT THEY ASK ◄
④ PAY ATTENTION
(FOR WITNESS
STATEMENT)

THE WORD
COLOUR IS WRITTEN
ON THIS CAMERA
TO SEE IF THE
PEOPLE ARE
COLOURED?

COLOUR

WATCHMAKER FRITS HUND STARTED HIS OWN
BUSINESS IN 1947 IN HIS ATTIC - AFTER A
ROW WITH HIS BOSS WHO REFUSED TO GIVE HIM
TIME OFF TO REGISTER HIS NEWBORN SON
AT THE TOWNHALL   GERARD?

BUILT-IN
SPOTLIGHTS

WOODEN   FROM
JEWELLERY STOCKROOM

GREENISH
NEON LIGHT

DESIRE

SILVER
CHAINS

LINK CHAIN
€ 390,-

AJAX
ALARM

F. HUN

THIS IS
WHERE FR
ALWAYS
SAT, PEOPLE
WOULD SEE
AS THEY
ENTERED
THE SHOP
THE DOOR W
ALWAYS OPE
THAT'S HOW
WANTED IT.

CASIO SPORTWATCHES

CLOCKS

SAFE

SCREEN

DORA

SILVER-PLATED
BEAR

ALL CLOCKS
ARE SET AT TEN
PAST TEN: SMILING
FACE

PIN   TILL

RULES ABOUT REPAIRS
AND EXCHANGE, AND
PIERCINGS ONLY WHEN
EARLOBES ARE BIG ENOUGH

BLING
BLING

WEDDING RINGS!
(DUMMIES) RINGS ARE
MADE TO MEASURE.
MOROCCANS OFTEN COLLECT
THEIR RING ON THE
WEDDING DAY ITSELF

TURKS ARE
THE MOST LOYAL
CUSTOMERS
(THEY OFTEN COME
BACK AND BRING THEIR
RELATIVES TOO...)

IN 1960 THE BUSINESS MOVED
HERE TO JAN EVERTSENSTRAAT 35
WEST AMSTERDAM
AFTER FRITS HUND DIED
HIS TWO SONS AND DAUGHTER
KEPT THE SHOP GOING

CARLA S
H

I'M SITTIN
HERE,
THERE'S
COFFEE AND
BISCUITS.
IT'S A BIT
COLD HE

XXL

TWO

JEWEL ROBBERY

In 2013, there were 250 robberies in
Amsterdam, targeting jewellers,
supermarkets and fast-food eateries.
The kid (he was 18) who shot Fred Hund
dead while robbing his jewellery store is
serving a fifteen year sentence. His DNA
was on the shoe he left behind in the shop.

OVERSIZED
WATCHES
(TO COMPENSATE?)
NOW IN FASHION

THE 1960s AN 70s WERE THE
BEST PERIOD. ALL THREE HAD A
COMPANY CAR. IN THE 1980s
THE BUSINESS DECLINED BECAUSE
THE NEIGHBOORHOOD CHANGED
(PEOPLE HAD CARS AND MOVED
OUT OF THE CITY)

COFFEE

ON 22 NOVEMBER A REPORT ON CRIMINAL ATTACKS IN THE NETHERLANDS APPEARED CONCLUDING THAT 16 OUT OF EVERY 100 ATTACKERS ARE JAILED. POLICE. THE COURTS AND LOCAL AUTHORITIES NEED TO COOPERATE MORE.
THE MINISTER IS DETERMINED TO REDUCE THE NUMBER OF ATTACKS BY IMPOSING HARDER PUNISHMENTS.

WILL IT WORK?
DO ROBBERS MAKE RATIONAL CALCULATIONS?

IT WAS ONLY WHEN GERARD SAW THE REPORT ON THE TV THAT HE REALISED THE INTRUDERS HAD BEEN WEARING RAINCOATS (IT WASN'T RAINING THAT DAY)

POLICE HAVE FILM OF THE ATTACK

56

CARLA HUND SAYS SHE IS A REAL PEOPLES PERSON, SHE KNOWS WHAT CUSTOMERS WANT... HOW? BY STOCKING FASHIONABLE BRANDS.

AIRCONDITIONING OLD-FASHIONED MODEL

OFF

GUESS

THIS WATCH COSTS: € 200,-

THEY ALSO COME WITH A SWISS MECHANISM (MORE EXPENSIVE)

THIS IS THE WINDOW TO THE REPAIR ROOM GERARD REMOVED THE GLASS SO HE COULD HEAR WHAT WAS GOING ON IN THE SHOP

SWITCH FOR AIR-CONDITIONING

ZODIAC SIGNS 14 CARATS

TW STC

GOLD BUDDHA REDUCED FROM €370 TO €220 - LAST CHANCE TO BUY!

LOCK

UPGRADE DIAMONDS THAT NO LONGER UPGRADE

ONE BALL OF PAPER

SALE TW-S

CHARM BRACELETS MY SISTER HAD ONE TOO 30 YEARS AGO.

THIS IS WHERE THE INTRUDER LEFT HIS SHOE (NIKE AIR SIZE 8)

FOR CHILDREN TO PLAY WITH

ON SATURDAY, 27 NOVEMBER THE SHOP OPENS FOR ONE LAST TIME WITH A CLOSING SALE!

RED (SOFT) CHAIRS

FRED TOOK SOME PERSUADING (THE TABLE)

IT WAS CARLA WHO THOUGHT OF HAVING A TABLE IN THE MIDDLE OF THE SHOP (REASSURING FOR CUSTOMERS)

THE FORENSIC INSTITUTE SAYS YOU CAN DISTIL A DNA PROFILE FROM A SHOE

I BOUGHT THE SILVER-PLATED BEAR FOR MY SON

BISCUITS

GERARD

SITS HERE

WHILE WE TALK, PEOPLE COME IN OFF THE STREET TO OFFER CONDOLENCES A MOROCCAN NEIGHBOUR EMBRACES EVERYONE

AFTER FIRING THE GUN, THE INTRUDERS FLEE WITHOUT TAKING ANYTHING. THEN GERARD SEES HIS BROTHER LYING OUTSIDE. THE 66-YEAR OLD FRED HUND IS SHOT IN HIS STOMACH AND DIES.

THE ATTACK LASTED 30 SECONDS

EXIT

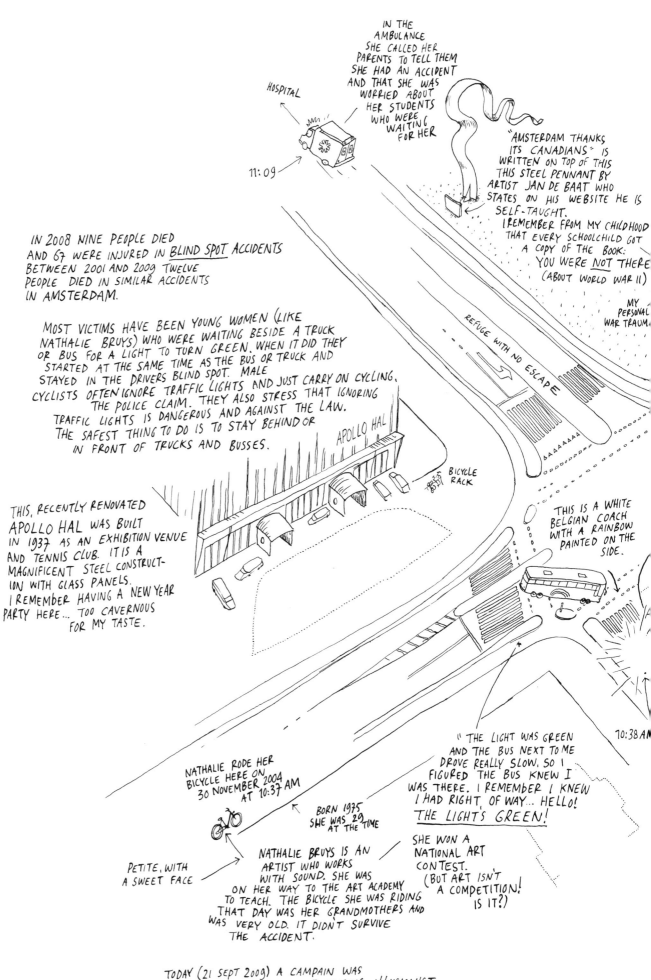

IN THE AMBULANCE SHE CALLED HER PARENTS TO TELL THEM SHE HAD AN ACCIDENT AND THAT SHE WAS WORRIED ABOUT HER STUDENTS WHO WERE WAITING FOR HER

HOSPITAL

11:09

"AMSTERDAM THANKS ITS CANADIANS" IS WRITTEN ON TOP OF THIS THIS STEEL PENNANT BY ARTIST JAN DE BAAT WHO STATES ON HIS WEBSITE HE IS SELF-TAUGHT. I REMEMBER FROM MY CHILDHOOD THAT EVERY SCHOOLCHILD GOT A COPY OF THE BOOK: YOU WERE NOT THERE (ABOUT WORLD WAR II)

MY PERSONAL WAR TRAUM

IN 2008 NINE PEOPLE DIED AND 67 WERE INJURED IN BLIND SPOT ACCIDENTS BETWEEN 2001 AND 2009 TWELVE PEOPLE DIED IN SIMILAR ACCIDENTS IN AMSTERDAM.

MOST VICTIMS HAVE BEEN YOUNG WOMEN (LIKE NATHALIE BRUYS) WHO WERE WAITING BESIDE A TRUCK OR BUS FOR A LIGHT TO TURN GREEN. WHEN IT DID THEY STARTED AT THE SAME TIME AS THE BUS OR TRUCK AND STAYED IN THE DRIVERS BLIND SPOT. MALE CYCLISTS OFTEN IGNORE TRAFFIC LIGHTS AND JUST CARRY ON CYCLING. THE POLICE CLAIM. THEY ALSO STRESS THAT IGNORING TRAFFIC LIGHTS IS DANGEROUS AND AGAINST THE LAW. THE SAFEST THING TO DO IS TO STAY BEHIND OR IN FRONT OF TRUCKS AND BUSSES.

REFUGE WITH NO ESCAPE

APOLLO HAL

BICYCLE RACK

THIS IS A WHITE BELGIAN COACH WITH A RAINBOW PAINTED ON THE SIDE.

THIS, RECENTLY RENOVATED APOLLO HAL WAS BUILT IN 1937 AS AN EXHIBITION VENUE AND TENNIS CLUB. IT IS A MAGNIFICENT STEEL CONSTRUCT-ION WITH GLASS PANELS. I REMEMBER HAVING A NEW YEAR PARTY HERE... TOO CAVERNOUS FOR MY TASTE.

10:38 AM

" THE LIGHT WAS GREEN AND THE BUS NEXT TO ME DROVE REALLY SLOW. SO I FIGURED THE BUS KNEW I WAS THERE. I REMEMBER I KNEW I HAD RIGHT OF WAY... HELLO! THE LIGHT'S GREEN!

NATHALIE RODE HER BICYCLE HERE ON 30 NOVEMBER 2004 AT 10:37 AM

BORN 1975 SHE WAS 29 AT THE TIME

PETITE, WITH A SWEET FACE

NATHALIE BRUYS IS AN ARTIST WHO WORKS WITH SOUND. SHE WAS ON HER WAY TO THE ART ACADEMY TO TEACH. THE BICYCLE SHE WAS RIDING THAT DAY WAS HER GRANDMOTHERS AND WAS VERY OLD. IT DIDN'T SURVIVE THE ACCIDENT.

SHE WON A NATIONAL ART CONTEST. (BUT ART ISN'T A COMPETITION! IS IT?)

TODAY (21 SEPT 2009) A CAMPAIN WAS LAUNCHED ON DUTCH TV FEATURING ILLUSIONIST HANS KLOK TO HIGHLIGHT THE DANGERS TO CYCLISTS WHO SHARE THE ROADS WITH CARS AND TRUCKS
→ SEE WWW.DODEHOEK.NL

74

In the last three years, 51 people drowned in Amsterdam's canals. Most were men, and drunk: they fell in while peeing and were unable to get back out. Another typical Amsterdam accident is cyclists in a truck's blind spot: usually it's young women who get caught and run over like this.

MARTIJN

A FRIEND OF MINE LIVED HERE AT THE GOLD COAST IN A GIGANTIC HOUSE. HIS FATHER WAS SOMEBODY IMPORTANT AT HEINEKEN.

MY FRIEND DIED YOUNG. HE JUMPED IN FRONT OF A TRAIN — HE SMOKED A LOT OF JOINTS

VERY EXPENSIVE HOUSES

STADION WEG

DOG (SHIT) FIELD

ALMOST 4 METERS HIGH!

← THIS BRONZE GIANTS STAND GUARD IN FRONT OF APOLLO HOUSE FORMERLY HOUSING THE SOCIAL INSURANCE.

THIS BUILDING WAS CALLED THE OCEAN STEAMER (SHIP)

EMPEROR AUGUSTUS' PATRON GOD.

NEXT MONTH WILL BE THE FIVE YEAR ANNIVERSARY OF THE ACCIDENT. HOW HAS MY LIFE CHANGED?

"I STILL CAN'T DANCE, AND THE INSURANCE COMPANY HAS BEEN GIVING ME A HARD TIME WORKING OUT WHAT MY INCOME WAS AS I'M AN ARTIST. SINCE THE ACCIDENT I HAVEN'T BEEN ABLE TO WALK FOR MORE THAN ONE HOUR (THAT'S REALLY THE LIMIT) I CAN ONLY WEAR WIDE PANTS, JEANS ARE TOO ROUGH TO WEAR AS THE SKIN ON MY LEGS IS STILL TOO SENSITIVE."

SCULPTURE FADED SANDSTONE (SOUR RAIN)

THIS PRIMAL SCREAM (LIKE AN ANIMAL) SAVED HER LIFE (SOUND ARTIST)

AAAAHHH

"I CAN'T REMEMBER HOW I ENDED UP UNDER THE BUS. I DO REMEMBER SCREAMING REALLY LOUDLY AND THAT THE BUS CAME TO A STOP ON TOP OF ME

HERE A MAN MOTIONED TO THE BUS DRIVER TO BACK UP. THE BUSDRIVER DIDN'T KNOW WHAT WAS GOING ON.

APOLLO LAAN

"WHEN THE BUS BACKED UP THE PAIN OVERWHELMED ME. THE PRESSURE OF THE WHEELS ON MY LEGS STOPPED, THIRTY CENTIMETERS MORE AND I WOULD HAVE BEEN DEAD

"LOOKING DOWN AT MY LEGS I SAW MY MUSCLES AND LOT OF YELLOWISH TISSUE AND BLOOD UNDERNEATH. MY WHITE BOOTS WERE STILL THERE AS IF NOTHING HAD HAPPENED I THOUGHT I LOST MY LEGS."

10:54 AM THE FIRST THING THE AMBULANCE MAN ASKED WETHER I COULD WIGGLE MY TOES. I SAID I COULD. HE HELD HIS THUMBS UP AND SAID. "GREAT" THEY GAVE ME A SHOT OF MORPHINE AND WRAPPED ME IN AN ALUMINIUM FOIL BLANKET.

I (JAN ROTHUIZEN) WAS HERE AGAIN WITH NATHALIE ON 21 AUGUST 2008 AT 12:48 AM

THIS IS AN ARTWORK BY TOM CLAASSEN A SOFT CAR TIPPED ON ITS SIDE THE WORK IS ENTITLED "CAR CRASH" IT'S PART OF A SCULPTURE ROUTE, ORGANISED BY DUTCH ACTOR/COMEDIAN MICHIEL ROMEYN.

"A WELL DRESSED WOMAN KNELT BESIDE ME AND HELD MY HAND, SHE HAD BIG BROWN EYES AND I REMEMBER THINKING.. PLEASE, STAY AND KEEP LOOKING AT ME, PLEASE DON'T GO.... SUDDENLY I FELT EXTREMELY COLD AND STARTED SHIVERING. IT SEEMED AS IF I HAD BEEN LYING THERE FOR AT LEAST HALF AN HOUR. THERE WAS ANOTHER MAN WHO CAME TO LOOK. I STILL WONDER IF THIS WAS THE DRIVER. I NEVER SAW HIM AGAIN THE WOMAN STAYED AND HELD MY HAND UNTIL THE AMBULANCE ARRIVED."

THE CHURCH GAINED ITS PRESENT SHAPE (AND SIZE) AROUND <u>1500</u> INSIDE IT LOOKED QUITE DIFFERENT THERE WERE LOTS OF CHAPELS AND IT WAS COLOURFUL AND CROWDED, LIKE A <u>FAIR</u>.

JOHANN SEBASTIAN BACH WAS INFLUENCED BY

<u>SWEELINCK</u>, THEN 15 YEARS OLD. BECAME THE ORGAN PLAYER HERE IN 1577

HE DIED WHEN HE WAS 59 AND WAS BURIED IN THIS CHURCH.

HE WAS FAMOUS FOR HIS IMPROVISATIONS.

IN THE RENAISSANCE CONCERTS ATTRACTED LOTS OF PEOPLE

LANCET WINDOW

SHIPBUILDING TECHNIQUES

LOOKS LIKE HULL A SH

PAINTING FROM 1421 (THE OLDEST)

THE CHURCH EMPLOYED A PASTOR (OR A PRIEST) BUT ALSO DOGCHASERS (THEY CHASED THE PROSTITUTES OUT AS WELL)

HAND-CUT

THE WHITE STONES OF THE OUTER WALL ARE FROM BENTHEIM (180 KILOMETRES AWAY FROM HERE)

THE BIG ORGAN

THERE WERE 39 ALTARS

BEFORE THE PROTESTANT TAKE OVER (1578) THIS WAS THE BAPTISTRY IN 1684 THE BURGOMASTER HAD IT MADE INTO HIS FAMILY GRAVE

ENTRANCE

CHOIR ORGAN PAINTING DATES FR 1650

REMBRANDTS SASKIA IS THE MOST FAMOUS (DEAD) WOMAN OF AMSTERDAM AFTER ANNE FRANK

SASKIA'S GRAVE

SCALE 1:18

THE SHEER SIZE OF THIS SCALE MODEL MADE THE REAL THING REDUNDANT

THESE ARE PEWS DURING THE CHURCH SERVICE ON SUNDAY JANUARY 20TH 2013

THERE ARE ABOUT 70 PEOPLE

THE PASTOR (WITH BLOND HAIR) EXPLAINS HOW JESUS TURNED WATER INTO WINE AND WONDERS WHAT THIS HAS TO DO WITH US.

A YEAR BEFORE THE OTTOMAN EMPIRE WAS FOUNDED

AROUND 1300 THE LOCAL FISHERMEN FOUNDED A WOODEN CHAPEL HERE

ARE STILL VERY SUPERSTITIOUS

THE GRAVESTONE FLOOR UNDULATES.

I DON'T UNDERSTAND EVERYTHING DURING THE SERVICE BUT I DO FIND IT BEAUTIFUL. (IS THAT ALRIGHT?)

6 YEARS LATER THE CHURCH WAS CONSECRATED

IN 1951 THE CHURCH WAS CLOSED BECAUSE IT WAS ABOUT TO <u>COLLAPSE!</u>

WAS THE LIGHT THAT BEAUTIFUL ALREADY?

IN THE SUMMER MONTHS TOURISTS MAKE A LITTLE EXTRA MONEY BY GUIDING OTHER TOURISTS AROUND. DO <u>NOT</u> BELIEVE EVERYTHING THEY SAY.

A MAJOR RENOVATION BEGINS

HOUSE IN A HOUSE

ABOUT 150.000 VISITORS A YEAR

NOW A FOUNDATION

OF THE CHURCH

WHEAT MERCHANTS CHAPEL

BARGE-MASTERS CHAPEL

CUTT CHO

HAMBURGER CHAPEL

LADY CHAPEL

ST GEORGE'S CHAPEL

HERE IS A CUPBOARD, THE CHURCH RECENTLY SWITCHED TO HIGH CURRENT POWER SUPPLY.

HANNY (58) RUNS THE TICKET DESK SHE USED TO SELL TICKETS ON THE TRAM.

FIRST

NORTH AISLE

NAVE

MOST VISITORS WANT TO KNOW WHERE (REMBRANDTS) SASKIA IS BURIED.

SOUTH AISLE

SMA CHAP

HOUSEBOUND CHAPEL

I (JAN ROTHUIZEN) WAS HERE IN JANUARY 2013. THERE WERE LOTS OF TOURISTS FROM EASTERN EUROPE (<u>NEW TREND!</u>)

ENTRANCE TOWER

BAPTISTRY

LYSBETH GAVEN CHAPEL

CHURCH WARDEN'S OFFICE

OUDE KERK

Amsterdam's oldest building is quiet and empty inside. That makes it harder to imagine how it must once have looked like a Hindu temple, full of bright colours, incense and music, instead of the cerebral tranquillity that reigns today.

CITY
GATE

OUTBOUND

TY
TES

In the 21st century, Amsterdam became a metropolitan
region with a population
of 2.3 million. Instead of
city walls, there are regional
links, while the gates through
which people entered and
left are now scattered about
the metropolis.

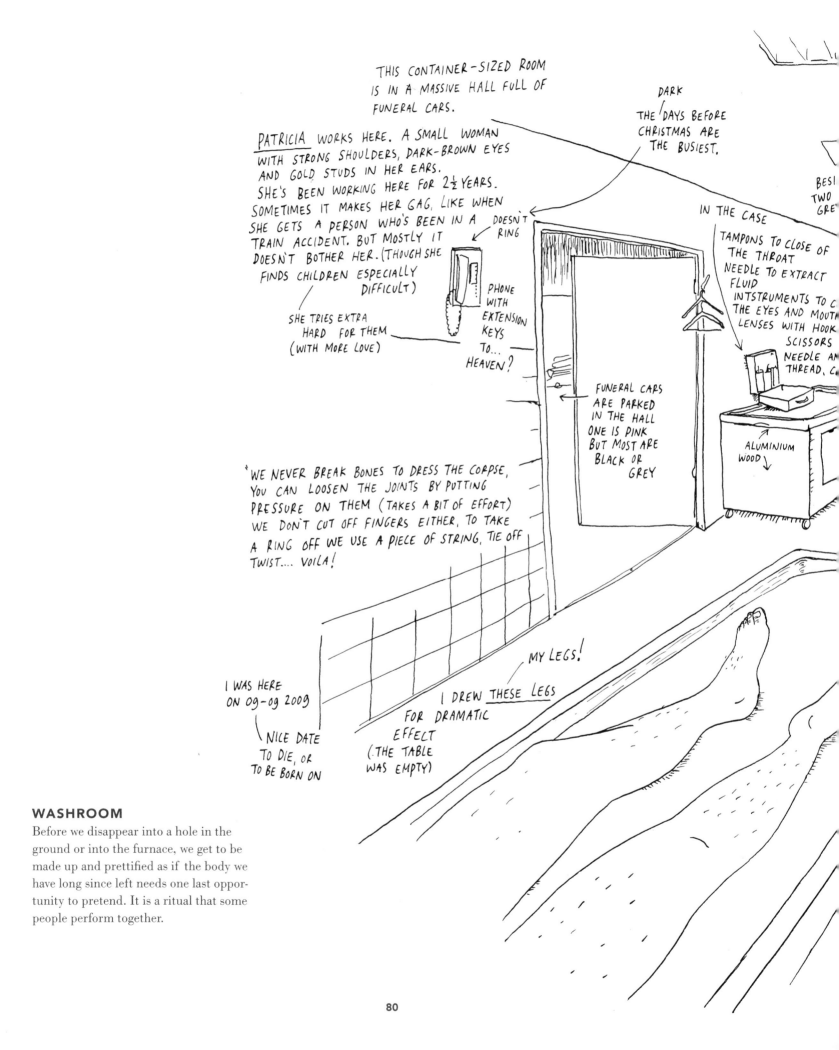

WASHROOM

Before we disappear into a hole in the ground or into the furnace, we get to be made up and prettified as if the body we have long since left needs one last opportunity to pretend. It is a ritual that some people perform together.

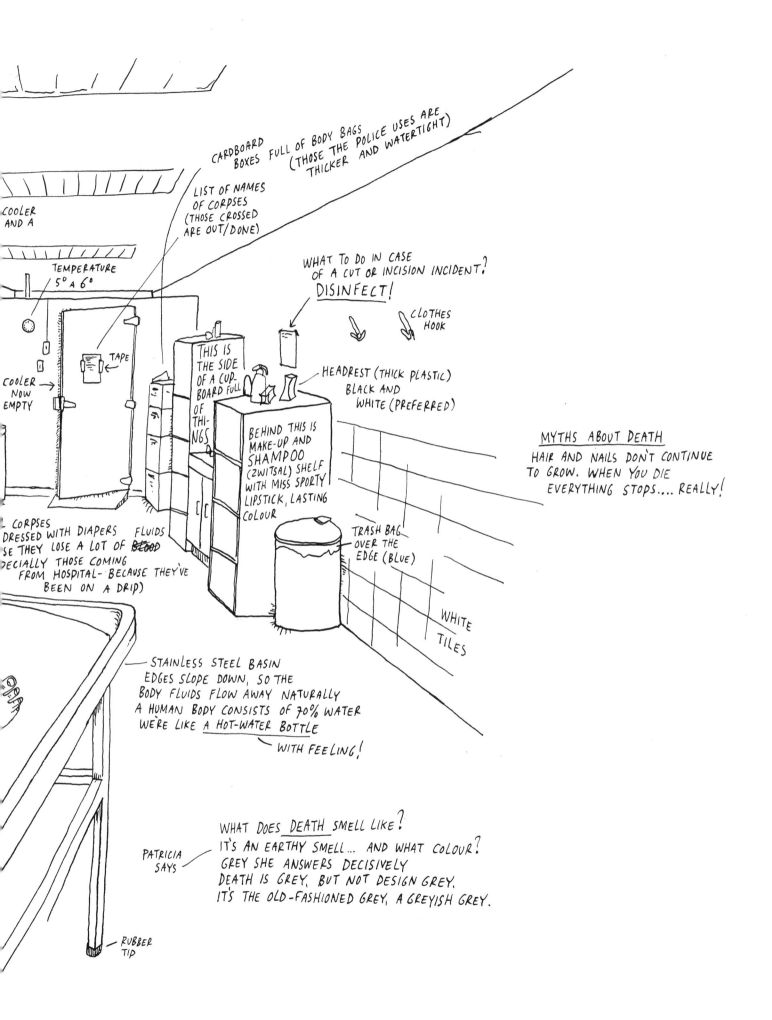

CARDBOARD BOXES FULL OF BODY BAGS (THOSE THE POLICE USES ARE THICKER AND WATERTIGHT)

LIST OF NAMES OF CORPSES (THOSE CROSSED ARE OUT/DONE)

COOLER AND A

TEMPERATURE 5° A 6°

WHAT TO DO IN CASE OF A CUT OR INCISION INCIDENT? DISINFECT!

CLOTHES HOOK

TAPE

COOLER NOW EMPTY

THIS IS THE SIDE OF A CUP-BOARD FULL OF THI-NGS

HEADREST (THICK PLASTIC) BLACK AND WHITE (PREFERRED)

MYTHS ABOUT DEATH
HAIR AND NAILS DON'T CONTINUE TO GROW. WHEN YOU DIE EVERYTHING STOPS.... REALLY!

BEHIND THIS IS MAKE-UP AND SHAMPOO (ZWITSAL) SHELF WITH MISS SPORTY LIPSTICK, LASTING COLOUR

CORPSES DRESSED WITH DIAPERS FLUIDS SE THEY LOSE A LOT OF ~~BLOOD~~ ECIALLY THOSE COMING FROM HOSPITAL- BECAUSE THEY'VE BEEN ON A DRIP)

TRASH BAG OVER THE EDGE (BLUE)

WHITE TILES

STAINLESS STEEL BASIN
EDGES SLOPE DOWN, SO THE BODY FLUIDS FLOW AWAY NATURALLY
A HUMAN BODY CONSISTS OF 70% WATER
WE'RE LIKE A HOT-WATER BOTTLE
⌐ WITH FEELING!

WHAT DOES DEATH SMELL LIKE?
IT'S AN EARTHY SMELL... AND WHAT COLOUR?
PATRICIA SAYS
GREY SHE ANSWERS DECISIVELY
DEATH IS GREY, BUT NOT DESIGN GREY.
IT'S THE OLD-FASHIONED GREY, A GREYISH GREY.

RUBBER TIP

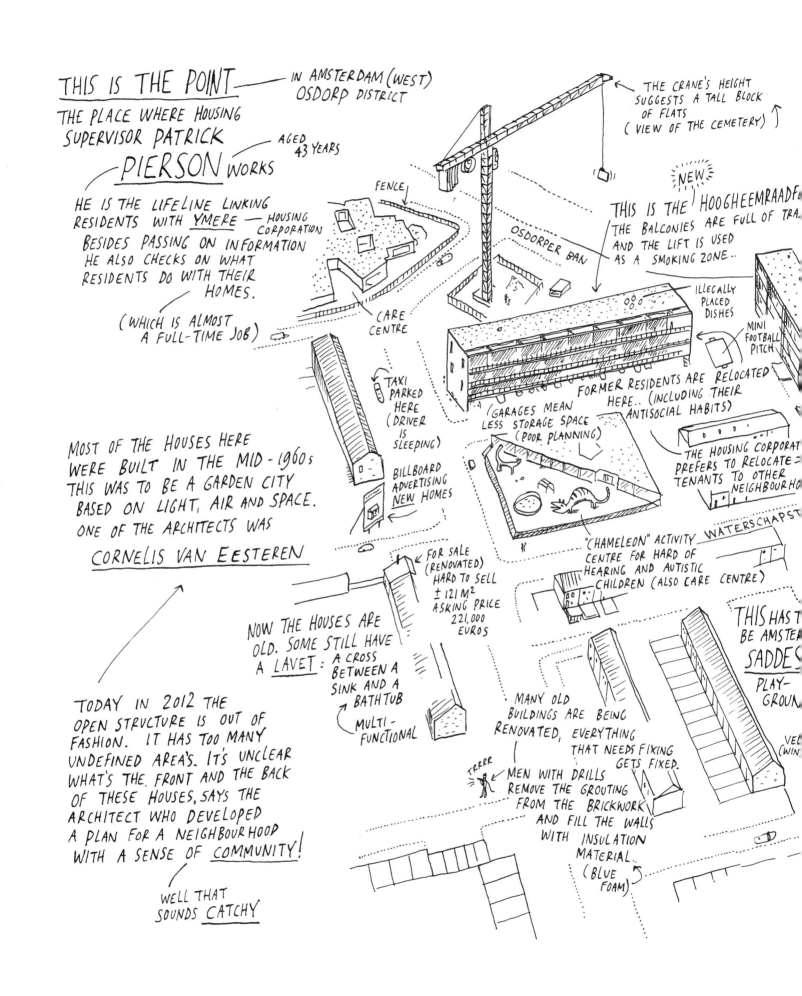

THIS IS THE POINT — IN AMSTERDAM (WEST) OSDORP DISTRICT

THE PLACE WHERE HOUSING SUPERVISOR PATRICK PIERSON WORKS — AGED 43 YEARS

HE IS THE LIFELINE LINKING RESIDENTS WITH YMERE — HOUSING CORPORATION BESIDES PASSING ON INFORMATION HE ALSO CHECKS ON WHAT RESIDENTS DO WITH THEIR HOMES.

(WHICH IS ALMOST A FULL-TIME JOB)

MOST OF THE HOUSES HERE WERE BUILT IN THE MID-1960s THIS WAS TO BE A GARDEN CITY BASED ON LIGHT, AIR AND SPACE. ONE OF THE ARCHITECTS WAS

CORNELIS VAN EESTEREN

TODAY IN 2012 THE OPEN STRUCTURE IS OUT OF FASHION. IT HAS TOO MANY UNDEFINED AREA'S. IT'S UNCLEAR WHAT'S THE FRONT AND THE BACK OF THESE HOUSES, SAYS THE ARCHITECT WHO DEVELOPED A PLAN FOR A NEIGHBOURHOOD WITH A SENSE OF COMMUNITY!

WELL THAT SOUNDS CATCHY

FENCE

OSDORPER BAN

CARE CENTRE

TAXI PARKED HERE (DRIVER IS SLEEPING)

BILLBOARD ADVERTISING NEW HOMES

NOW THE HOUSES ARE OLD. SOME STILL HAVE A LAVET: A CROSS BETWEEN A SINK AND A BATHTUB

MULTI-FUNCTIONAL

FOR SALE (RENOVATED) HARD TO SELL ± 121 M² ASKING PRICE 221,000 EUROS

THE CRANE'S HEIGHT SUGGESTS A TALL BLOCK OF FLATS (VIEW OF THE CEMETERY)

NEW

THIS IS THE HOOGHEEMRAADF... THE BALCONIES ARE FULL OF TRA... AND THE LIFT IS USED AS A SMOKING ZONE..

ILLEGALLY PLACED DISHES

MINI FOOTBALL PITCH

FORMER RESIDENTS ARE RELOCATED HERE.. (INCLUDING THEIR ANTISOCIAL HABITS)

(GARAGES MEAN LESS STORAGE SPACE (POOR PLANNING)

THE HOUSING CORPORAT... PREFERS TO RELOCATE = TENANTS TO OTHER NEIGHBOURHO...

"CHAMELEON" ACTIVITY CENTRE FOR HARD OF HEARING AND AUTISTIC CHILDREN (ALSO CARE CENTRE)

WATERSCHAPST...

THIS HAS T... BE AMSTE... SADDES... PLAY-GROUN...

VEL (WIN...

MANY OLD BUILDINGS ARE BEING RENOVATED, EVERYTHING THAT NEEDS FIXING GETS FIXED.

TRRRR

MEN WITH DRILLS REMOVE THE GROUTING FROM THE BRICKWORK AND FILL THE WALLS WITH INSULATION MATERIAL (BLUE FOAM)

END OF THE LINE
This is where the tram turns in a circle
and heads back into town. Osdorp is one
of the garden cities that were built in the
1950s and 60s to be green and spacious.
It is long past its prime and is
getting refurbished.

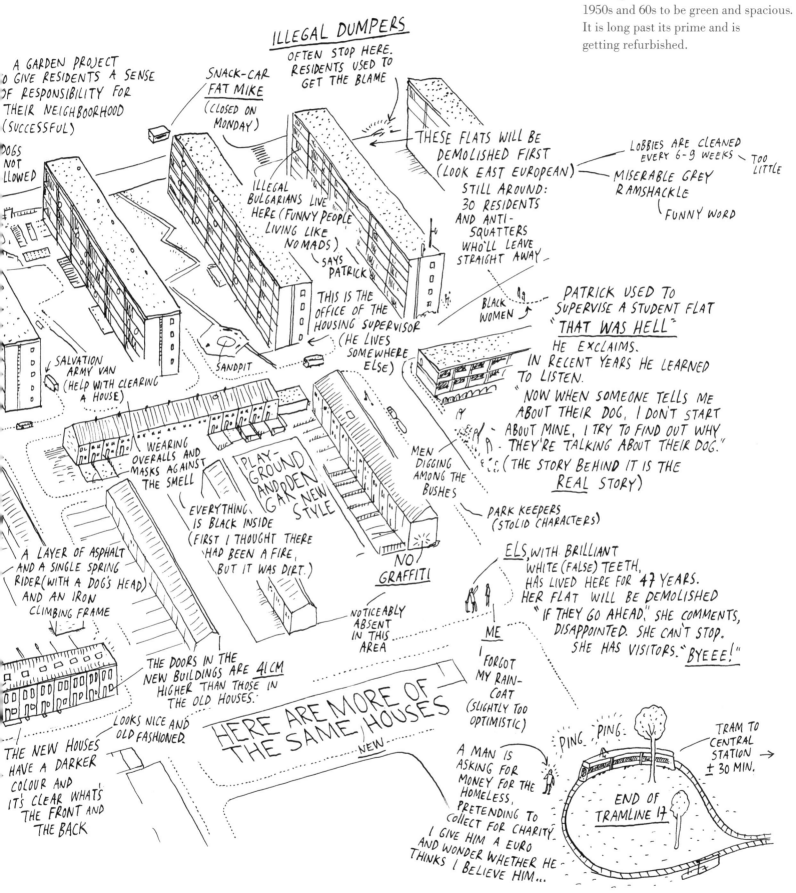

A GARDEN PROJECT
TO GIVE RESIDENTS A SENSE
OF RESPONSIBILITY FOR
THEIR NEIGHBOORHOOD
(SUCCESSFUL)

DOGS
NOT
LLOWED

SNACK-CAR
FAT MIKE
(CLOSED ON
MONDAY)

ILLEGAL DUMPERS
OFTEN STOP HERE.
RESIDENTS USED TO
GET THE BLAME

ILLEGAL
BULGARIANS LIVE
HERE (FUNNY PEOPLE
LIVING LIKE
NOMADS)
SAYS
PATRICK

THESE FLATS WILL BE
DEMOLISHED FIRST
(LOOK EAST EUROPEAN)
STILL AROUND:
30 RESIDENTS
AND ANTI-
SQUATTERS
WHO'LL LEAVE
STRAIGHT AWAY

LOBBIES ARE CLEANED
EVERY 6-9 WEEKS
TOO
LITTLE
MISERABLE GREY
RAMSHACKLE
FUNNY WORD

THIS IS THE
OFFICE OF THE
HOUSING SUPERVISOR
(HE LIVES
SOMEWHERE
ELSE)

BLACK
WOMEN

PATRICK USED TO
SUPERVISE A STUDENT FLAT
"THAT WAS HELL"
HE EXCLAIMS.
IN RECENT YEARS HE LEARNED
TO LISTEN.
"NOW WHEN SOMEONE TELLS ME
ABOUT THEIR DOG, I DON'T START
ABOUT MINE, I TRY TO FIND OUT WHY
THEY'RE TALKING ABOUT THEIR DOG."
(THE STORY BEHIND IT IS THE
REAL STORY)

SALVATION
ARMY VAN
(HELP WITH CLEARING
A HOUSE)

SANDPIT

WEARING
OVERALLS AND
MASKS AGAINST
THE SMELL

PLAY-
GROUND
AND GARDEN
NEW
STYLE

MEN
DIGGING
AMONG THE
BUSHES

PARK KEEPERS
(STOLID CHARACTERS)

EVERYTHING
IS BLACK INSIDE
(FIRST I THOUGHT THERE
HAD BEEN A FIRE,
BUT IT WAS DIRT.)

NO
GRAFFITI

A LAYER OF ASPHALT
AND A SINGLE SPRING
RIDER (WITH A DOG'S HEAD)
AND AN IRON
CLIMBING FRAME

NOTICEABLY
ABSENT
IN THIS
AREA

ME
I FORGOT
MY RAIN-
COAT
(SLIGHTLY TOO
OPTIMISTIC)

ELS, WITH BRILLIANT
WHITE (FALSE) TEETH,
HAS LIVED HERE FOR 47 YEARS.
HER FLAT WILL BE DEMOLISHED
"IF THEY GO AHEAD," SHE COMMENTS,
DISAPPOINTED. SHE CAN'T STOP.
SHE HAS VISITORS. "BYEEE!"

THE DOORS IN THE
NEW BUILDINGS ARE 41CM
HIGHER THAN THOSE IN
THE OLD HOUSES.

LOOKS NICE AND
OLD FASHIONED.

HERE ARE MORE OF
THE SAME HOUSES
NEW

THE NEW HOUSES
HAVE A DARKER
COLOUR AND
IT'S CLEAR WHAT'S
THE FRONT AND
THE BACK

A MAN IS
ASKING FOR
MONEY FOR THE
HOMELESS,
PRETENDING TO
COLLECT FOR CHARITY.
I GIVE HIM A EURO
AND WONDER WHETHER HE
THINKS I BELIEVE HIM...

PING PING

END OF
TRAMLINE 17

TRAM TO
CENTRAL
STATION →
± 30 MIN.

BIRDS OF A FEATHER

When Surinam gained independence from Holland in 1975, many people left the country. Out of Surinams 819,000 citizens, around 327,000 live in Holland. Many settled in Southeast Amsterdam. They are Amsterdam's biggest ethnic group, followed by Moroccans and Turks.

THIS IS KRAKA - E - SEWA — MEANS "CARE" IN HINDI.
A PLACE WHERE SURINAMESE SENIORS WITH FIRST STAGES OF DEMENTIA OR OTHER MEMORY ISSUES CAN MEET
KRAKA IS SURINAMESE FOR "SUPPORT"
(SUPPORT FOR FAMILY AND CARE FOR CLIENT)

EX-TRACTOR (SILVER)

FRIDGE

RAKA

NO, THIS ISN'T SINTERKLAAS DECORATION ITS A PORTRAIT OF A CREOLE WOMAN IN TRADITIONAL COSTUME

HERE WE'RE BIRDS OF A FEATHER

THAT'S WHAT A MAN SAID WHO CAME HERE NOT THIS MAN

THERE'S A MAN SITTING ALONE HERE TODAY

BEHIND THIS DOOR HOBBY THINGS, BOOKS ON SURINAM, COATS AND BAGS

12.55 GRACE AND LUNCH

ANNE-ROSE (COORDINATOR) WAN A BIG TREE IN TH CENTRE OF THE RO SO EVERYONE COUL SIT UNDERNEATH LIKE IN SURINAME (BUT THEN... HOW TO KEEP IT CLEAN?

COLOUR-FULL TABLE CLOTH

I LEAVE MY BAG HERE BEHIND THIS DOOR

THERE'S A WOMAN SITTING IN THIS CHAIR WHO CAN'T SPEAK BUT IS HAVING LOTS OF FUN (LOUDLY)

EVERYTHING IS NEW AND CLEAN HERE

SO NO MICE

LEG AND FOOT REST

SOME PEOPLE WITH DEMENTIA LOSE THEIR SHOR TERM MEMORY AND SO THEY LIVE IN THE PAST AND BECOME NOSTALGIC WHICH IS A PSYCHOLOGIC CONDITION

THE KITCHEN IS JERRY'S DOMAIN, HE IS A NO-SALT COOK. SALT IS BAD FOR YOU INSTEAD OF SALT, HE USES FLAVOUR ENHANCER FAVOURITE DISH HERE IS CHOW-MIN (WITHOUT PORK) — RELAXED SORT

NURSE MURIEL JOKES THAT SHE'S HAPPY THIS WOMAN CAN'T SPEAK, BECAUSE OTHERWISE SHE'D NEVER STOP!

HERE IN SOUTH EAST AMSTERDAM

BESIDE THE FLATS FOR SURINAMESE SENIORS
(WITH FIRST STAGES OF DEMENTIA)
UPSTAIRS IN THIS BUILDING THERE ARE
SELF-CATERING FLATS FOR YOUNG ADULTS
WITH A LIGHT TO MODERATE INTELLECTUAL
DISABILITY.

AIR

THE STAR?
HOPE AND UNITY

GREEN IS FOR
THE LAND'S
FERTILITY

RED =
PROGRESS

WHITE =
PEACE
(IN BETWEEN)

SURINAME
BECAME A
REPUBLIC
IN 1975

FLAG

10.28
TENNIS
ON TV
(KIM
CLIJSTERS
WINS)

OLD GOSPEL SONGS
BY JIM REEVES ON THE
CD-PLAYER

WINDOW

COCONUT
(PLASTER)

POK

POK

CD +
RADIO

PAINTING
IN THE
CUPBOARD
IS THAT
ANTON
DE KOM?

DOLL

HERE JOAN'S SON
IS PLAYING A
COMPUTER GAME
PEEP PEEP PEEP

POLITICAL
ACTIVIST

OLD MEN ARE
TALKING (AND
ABOUT LAUGHING)
WOMEN

PICAL
-D-
-D-
RD

COM-
PULSORY
PLANT

10.50 THE
DAY STARTS
WITH A
TEXT FROM
THE BIBLE

LOOKS
NEW

AUNTIE TRACE
IS CUTTING AND
GLUEING PAPERCHAINS
FOR HER SON WHO IS
COMING OVER
FROM
SURINAM

WORD
PUZZLE

THIS MORNING WHILE I'M HERE
I REALISE THAT NOSTALGIA

CAN BE INFECTIOUS.... SUDDENLY
I WANT TO GO TO SURINAME TOO

I ASK ANN-ROSE HOW MUCH
A TICKET COSTS
(AROUND 1000 EUROS)

MY PLATE
I ATE IT
ALL

PEACE MISSION

Between 2006 and 2010, the Dutch sent 1,400 soldiers to Afghanistan. They were part of the International Security Assistance Force (ISAF). Their mission was to promote stability and security in Uruzgan province. Twenty Dutch soldiers died in all.

THIS IS TIMO SMEEHUIJZEN'S ROOM I WAS HERE ON 17 JUNE 2010, THREE YEARS AND THREE DAYS AFTER HE WAS KILLED IN A BOMB EXPLOSION IN URUZGAN, AFGHANISTAN WHILE SERVING AS A SOLDIER

TIMO HAD JU... TURNED 20...

CLOCK WITH REVERSE ORDER NUMERALS, NOT SURE IF THE HANDS TURN BACK TOO CLOCK HAS STOPPED

NINE CHILDREN ALSO DIED IN THAT EXPLOSION

WINDOW TO CORRIDOR

(CHEAP) SUNGLASSES

NIGHT BUS GUIDE

FRONT OF SPEAKER IS REMOVED (I USED TO DO THIS TOO)

FLUFFY TOY WEARING A SWEATER

IN THE BOOKCASE: THE SCARY BUS, BY PAUL VAN LOON. AND ALSO "IF I DIE IN A COMBAT ZONE BOX ME UP AND SEND ME HOME" AUTOBIOGRAPHY OF AN AMERICAN SOLDIER IN VIETNAM 1973

LOOKS STILL UNREAD

NO ENTRY (SIGN)

MEDALS (MINI MARATHON)

ROCKET (TOY)

FOLDER WITH CDS AND DVDS (LOTS OF HIP HOP)

AL PACINO SCARFACE

PHOTO OF GIRLFRIEND (MELODY KLAVER) SHE IS AN ACTRESS IN 2006 →

LAMP ON ROLLER-SKATE WHEELS

"LUKE" FROM STAR WARS)

PEN KNIFE

NOTE-PAD (EMPTY)

FRAME

SLIDING-DOOR

ARMY BAG. BEIGE (CAMOUFLAGE)

STAR WARS POSTER USED TO BE ON THE WALL. TIMO'S MOTHER TOOK IT DOWN RECENTLY. SHE ARGUED TIMO WOULD BE TOO OLD FOR THIS IN THE MEANTIME ANYWAY

BOYS STUFF: PADLOCK, FELT PENS AND CARDS

THERE WAS A COMPUTER

ORIGAMI BIRD

TIMO LEARNED TO MAKE THESE THOUGH HE WASN'T PARTICULARLY GOOD WITH HIS HANDS. HIS MOTHER SAYS.

TIMO SWAPPED THIS CATAPULT WITH A KID IN TARIN KOW... FOR A CAN OF COKE

MY VERY FIRST PHOTO ALBUM (BABY PICTURES)

1970 (WHITE PLASTIC) NEWSPAPER HOLDER (INCONGRUOUS)

SAVE THE CHILDREN FOLDERS. TIMO'S PARENTS AND FRIENDS HAVE COLLECTED MONEY TO BUILD A SCHOOL WHERE TIMO DIED. IT OPENED IN MARCH.

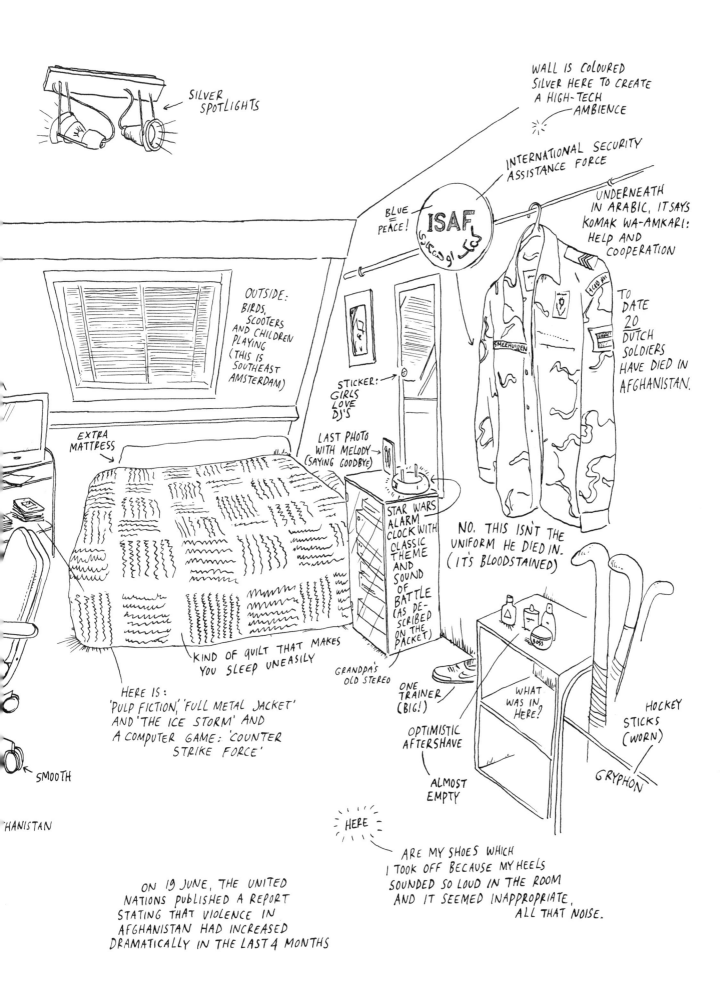

SILVER SPOTLIGHTS

WALL IS COLOURED SILVER HERE TO CREATE A HIGH-TECH AMBIENCE

INTERNATIONAL SECURITY ASSISTANCE FORCE

BLUE = PEACE!

ISAF
کمک او امکاري

UNDERNEATH IN ARABIC, IT SAYS KOMAK WA-AMKARI: HELP AND COOPERATION

TO DATE 20 DUTCH SOLDIERS HAVE DIED IN AFGHANISTAN.

OUTSIDE: BIRDS, SCOOTERS AND CHILDREN PLAYING (THIS IS SOUTHEAST AMSTERDAM)

EXTRA MATTRESS

STICKER: GIRLS LOVE DJ'S

LAST PHOTO WITH MELODY (SAYING GOODBYE)

STAR WARS ALARM CLOCK WITH CLASSIC THEME AND SOUND OF BATTLE (AS DESCRIBED ON THE PACKET)

NO. THIS ISN'T THE UNIFORM HE DIED IN. (IT'S BLOODSTAINED)

KIND OF QUILT THAT MAKES YOU SLEEP UNEASILY

GRANDPA'S OLD STEREO

ONE TRAINER (BIG!)

OPTIMISTIC AFTERSHAVE

WHAT WAS IN HERE?

HOCKEY STICKS (WORN)

GRYPHON

HERE IS: 'PULP FICTION', 'FULL METAL JACKET' AND 'THE ICE STORM' AND A COMPUTER GAME: 'COUNTER STRIKE FORCE'

SMOOTH

HANISTAN

ALMOST EMPTY

HERE

ARE MY SHOES WHICH I TOOK OFF BECAUSE MY HEELS SOUNDED SO LOUD IN THE ROOM AND IT SEEMED INAPPROPRIATE, ALL THAT NOISE.

ON 19 JUNE, THE UNITED NATIONS PUBLISHED A REPORT STATING THAT VIOLENCE IN AFGHANISTAN HAD INCREASED DRAMATICALLY IN THE LAST 4 MONTHS

TO RIJKSMUSEUM

AND LEIDSEPLEIN

TO TRAM 2
TO CENTRAL STATION
TING TING

ODE
THIS WAS
CONCER
HALL
IN 183

FRESH HERRING

LIMP WRIST (GAY BARS)

SHOE SHOP

HARING

CLEANING GA
PARKS

SPECIAL OFFER

AMSTERDAM

4 BAGS FOR 10 EURO

SMELLS

THE CURL
PUBLIC URINAL FOR MEN

ATMOSPHERE (DAMPKRING)

BAG OF 10 TULIP BULBS

NOT MANY FRESH FLOWERS AT THIS MARKET (FOR TOURISTS)

SYMBOL OF DANCE (HOUSE) CULTURE

LATE 1980's

THE CLUB
ROXY
zzzz
WAS HERE

THIS SHOPPING MALL FEELS SUBURBAN

MINT TOWER

DONG DING

DONG DING

HEMA SAUSAGE

MAI
BONN

THE ROXY IS NOW A FASHION SHOP

CHILDHOOD MEMORIES FOR ME

HOCKEY CHIC (PINK POLO SHIRTS)

DRINK AND DRIVE

THIS WAS PART OF THE MEDIEVAL CITY WALL

MOTHER AND DAUGHTER SHOP TOGETHER

BEERBIKE

UN

LA LA

THIS IS A MOBILE BAR!

HELLO!

IN AMSTERDAM

MOST VISITORS ARE BETWEEN 21-30 (29%)

FITS UP TO 17 PERSONS (AND ENOUGH BEER)

THE DESIGNATED SOBER DRIVER THE

(RENT 450 EUROS)

ROKIN

Cattle dealers were still prodding livestock through the alleys to Ossenmarkt until well into the 17th century. Today it's not calves but around five million tourists and 16 million day-trippers who traipse around the historic inner city each year.

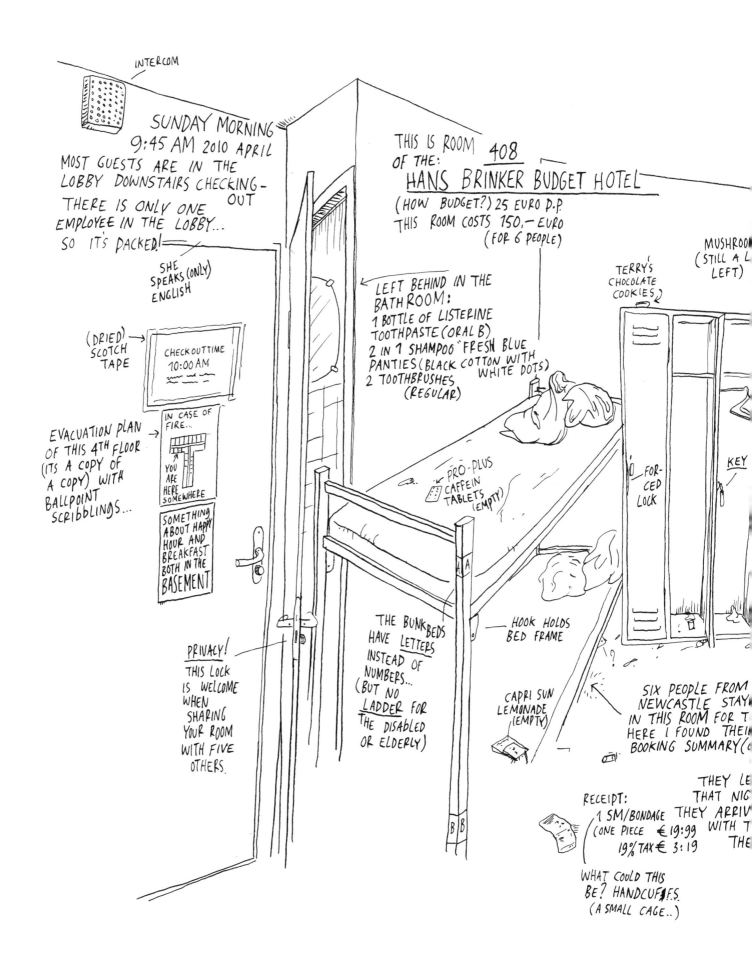

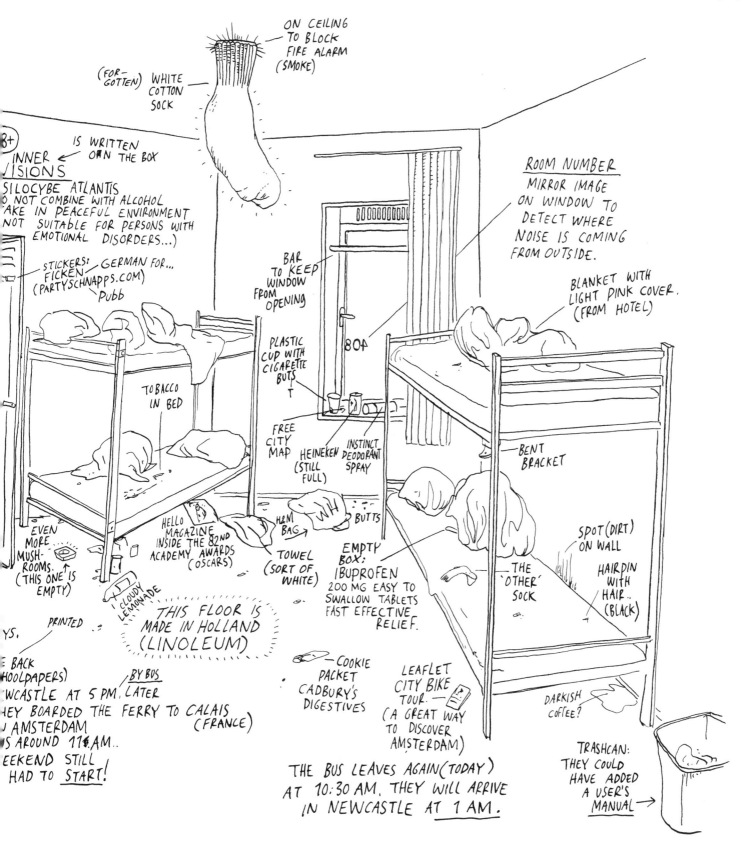

BUDGET HOTEL

Amsterdam is a favourite among people in their twenties. That is the biggest group of visitors. It is especially popular for stag and bachelors parties, with young grooms on a blow-out on their last night of freedom - a last smoke and a grope.

RECYCLED ENERGY

Amsterdam's refuse energy company says that there's no such thing as trash. And it's true that they turn 99.7 % of the city's rubbish into green electricity for trams and buses, and which provides city heating for entire neighbourhoods. But what about that tiny remnant, that last bit which refuses to be recycled?

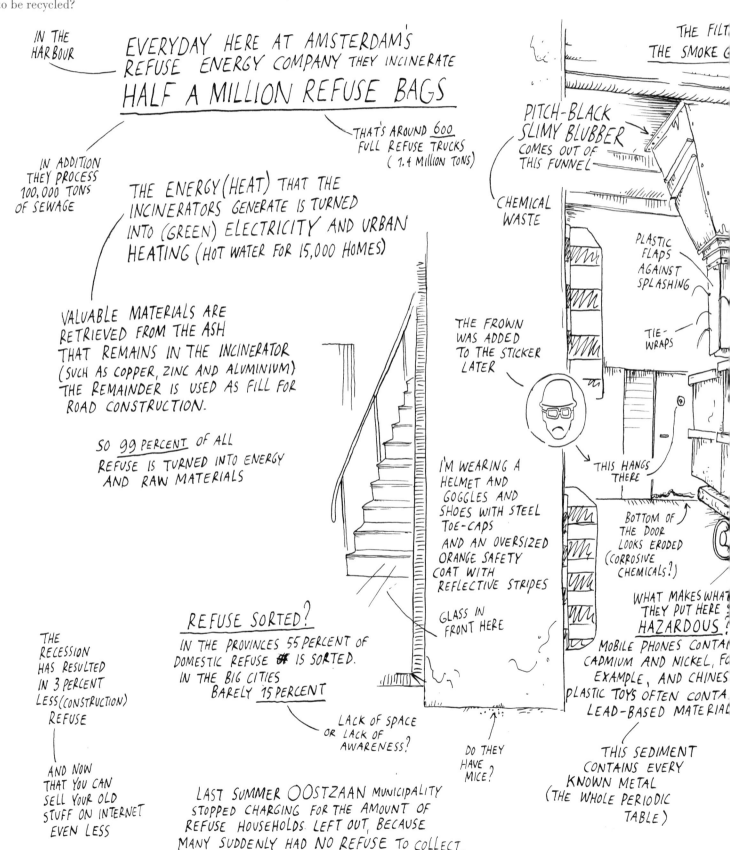

IN THE HARBOUR

EVERYDAY HERE AT AMSTERDAM'S REFUSE ENERGY COMPANY THEY INCINERATE **HALF A MILLION REFUSE BAGS**

THAT'S AROUND <u>600</u> FULL REFUSE TRUCKS (1.4 MILLION TONS)

IN ADDITION THEY PROCESS 100,000 TONS OF SEWAGE

THE ENERGY (HEAT) THAT THE INCINERATORS GENERATE IS TURNED INTO (GREEN) ELECTRICITY AND URBAN HEATING (HOT WATER FOR 15,000 HOMES)

VALUABLE MATERIALS ARE RETRIEVED FROM THE ASH THAT REMAINS IN THE INCINERATOR (SUCH AS COPPER, ZINC AND ALUMINIUM) THE REMAINDER IS USED AS FILL FOR ROAD CONSTRUCTION.

SO <u>99 PERCENT</u> OF ALL REFUSE IS TURNED INTO ENERGY AND RAW MATERIALS

THE RECESSION HAS RESULTED IN 3 PERCENT LESS (CONSTRUCTION) REFUSE

AND NOW THAT YOU CAN SELL YOUR OLD STUFF ON INTERNET EVEN LESS

<u>REFUSE SORTED?</u>
IN THE PROVINCES 55 PERCENT OF DOMESTIC REFUSE IS SORTED. IN THE BIG CITIES BARELY <u>15 PERCENT</u>

LACK OF SPACE OR LACK OF AWARENESS?

LAST SUMMER OOSTZAAN MUNICIPALITY STOPPED CHARGING FOR THE AMOUNT OF REFUSE HOUSEHOLDS LEFT OUT, BECAUSE MANY SUDDENLY HAD <u>NO REFUSE</u> TO COLLECT.

THE FROWN WAS ADDED TO THE STICKER LATER

I'M WEARING A HELMET AND GOGGLES AND SHOES WITH STEEL TOE-CAPS AND AN OVERSIZED ORANGE SAFETY COAT WITH REFLECTIVE STRIPES

GLASS IN FRONT HERE

DO THEY HAVE MICE?

THE FILT
THE SMOKE G

PITCH-BLACK SLIMY BLUBBER COMES OUT OF THIS FUNNEL

CHEMICAL WASTE

PLASTIC FLAPS AGAINST SPLASHING

TIE-WRAPS

THIS HANGS THERE

BOTTOM OF THE DOOR LOOKS ERODED (CORROSIVE CHEMICALS?)

WHAT MAKES WHAT THEY PUT HERE HAZARDOUS?

MOBILE PHONES CONTA CADMIUM AND NICKEL, F EXAMPLE, AND CHINES PLASTIC TOYS OFTEN CONTA LEAD-BASED MATERIAL

THIS SEDIMENT CONTAINS EVERY KNOWN METAL (THE WHOLE PERIODIC TABLE)

THIS IS THE ARSHOLE OF OUR CONSUMER SOCIETY.
THE PLACE WHERE THE REFUSE THAT CAN'T BE PROCESSED ANY FURTHER
COMES OUT. ## THE END OF THE CYCLE

HAUST OF
RIFICATION RESIDUE

ROLL-DOWN
SHUTTER
(DOESN'T
LOOK
USED)

DURING THE
HOLIDAYS THE
INCINERATOR
BURNS BETTER
BECAUSE PEOPLE
THROW AWAY MORE
FATTY FOODS

TURKEY AND
CHRISTMAS PIES

METAL
(BLUE)

FLORESCENT
LIGHT
(EVEN AT
CHRISTMAS)

THAT ONE PERCENT OF REFUSE
WHICH THIS ENERGY PLANT CAN'T
PROCESS IS GENERALLY REDUCED TO
A DRY SAND-LIKE MATERIAL AND
DEPOSITED IN OLD GERMAN MINE
SHAFTS.

WALL IS PAINTED
WHITE UP TO
HERE, TO DETECT
THE SPLASHES
PERHAPS?

STEEL
BUMPERS
FOR SAFETY?

RECYCLED
GALVANISED
STEEL CONTAINER

ORANGE
AND BLACK
(LIKE
BEES)

← SPLASHES

READY FOR
TRANSPORT
TO GERMANY
IN ROBUST
PLASTIC
SACKS.

TAPE
(HOLE?)

WAGON
WAS ONCE ORANGE
(AND PROUD)
NOW RUSTY BROWN
AND DISAPPOINTED

THE CONTENTS
OF THESE
CONTAINERS
GOES TO A TIP
FOR HAZARDOUS
CHEMICALS IN THE
MAAS ESTUARY

AEB AMSTERDAM

A RUBBER TIRE
MAY SOON BE A
UBBER TILE UNDER
SPRING RIDER

RECYCLING IS
(OFTEN) DOWN-CYCLING

AROUND 10 TRUCKS
A YEAR
(500 TONS)

THIS IS WHERE
PASTOR SAMUEL
FROM GHANA WORKS
IN A WHITE COAT WITH A
MASK, MOVING THESE BAGS
WITH A FORK-LIFT TRUCK

HE SOUNDS DARK AND LOUD
LIKE A REAL PASTOR

ACKNOWLEDGE-
MENTS

Some drawings in this book commissioned.
I want to thank the following:

Air Traffic Control The Netherlands / De Appel Arts Centre / ING Bank Amsterdam / Maritime Museum Rotterdam / Oude Kerk Foundation / The Physical Planning Department (DRO), Amsterdam / Rijks-museum Amsterdam / de Volkskrant / Ymere Housing Corporation

THANKS:
This book would have been impossible to make without the trust and assistance of the many people I have met over the past few years.

Karima Benali / Marije Braat / Ineke Brunt / Friso Broeksma / Nathalie Bruys / Centre for visual Arts Southeast Amsterdam / Karin van Dam / Dutch Council for Refugees / Barbara Van Erp / Ekmel foundation / Anne Frank Foundation / Chris Fruneaux / Arno Haijtema / Sammy Hemerik / Boris Hilberdink Gerard Hund / Onno Hogenaar / Roosje Klap / Mrs Kooy † / Chris Keulemans / Janneke Louman / Mirjam Konijn / Marieke Meijer / Cathy Hak / Julia van Mourik / Boris de Munnick / Nienke Nauta / Pepijn Reeser / Carla Rothuizen-De Vries / Jeroen Slot Ruud Smeehuijzen / Mo Veld / Roland van der Vorst

SOURCES:
Amsterdam.nl / ArchiNed / 1000 jaar Amsterdam, Fred Feddes / Bing Maps / The Department for Research and Statistics, (S+O) Amsterdam / Google Maps / Google Earth / De Grote Bosatlas / NRC Handelsblad / Het Parool / de Volkskrant / Wikipedia